# the *focus, fuel, & foliage* issue

Surprising Coffee Hacks — 74

Teaching Permaculture Through Art — 42

Air Plants — 24

# FEATURES

**12 Plants in the Classroom**

Why your students need them, and how to care for each recommended type

**64 Conscious Living**

Teacher-spouses sound off on balance, give advice for toxin-free living, and share how to navigate the tricky evening hours

**36 Building Wealth on a Teacher Salary**

Insights to help you plan for retirement, budgeting options for what you've got, and side gig suggestions for when it's not working

**28 Creativity and the Brain**

How to take advantage of diffused thinking

Teaching with creative approaches based on neuroscience

Bonus Fill-In Reflections 108

**48 Classroom Tour**
& back cover photography
Megan Rowe

**100 5 Ways to Style a Maxi Dress**

## CONTENTS

**98** Your Guide to Dry Brushing

**56** Productivity with your Cycle

**74** Spice Up Your All-Day-Long Drinks

**34** Rug Materials: Durability vs. Comfort

**88** Papercrafting & Bookbinding

**103** Teacher, Baker, Creator

**60** Peppermint Essential Oil Hacks

**8** Feedback Languages

### IN EVERY ISSUE

| | |
|---|---|
| From the Editor | 4 |
| Bell Work | 7 |
| Classroom Tour | 48 |
| Discover | 62 |
| Passing Notes | 72 |
| Mind of a Creator | 88 |
| Inspiration From... | 110 |

**24** All About Air Plants

**86** Paper's Possibilities!

*Mystery is at the heart of creativity. That, and surprise.* >> Julia Cameron

SNOWDAYMAGAZINE.COM | 3

## FROM THE EDITOR...

Teachers are passionate, hard working, and always have our career and our students front and center as a priority. We devote all our love and mental attention to those that matter to us. But we're also multi dimensional and have such vibrant, full lives outside the classroom. It's time to focus on the lifestyle aspect of a teacher's world. Because there's more to the story. Teachers are also brilliant, creative, and spiritual! There are so many facets that come together to make us the kind of people that can rock our jobs, love our students so fiercely, build a household and family, and still have passion left for crafty endeavors, spirituality, design, and relationships.

It's rare for a teacher to ever truly be "off the clock." But on a snow day, teachers get a minute to sit back and actually focus on themselves. We can nurture all the other aspects of our life and fill our souls with what re-energizes us. For some of us, that's a craft or hobby. For some, it's designing a beautiful home environment. For some, it's just a long soak with the bathroom door closed, a glass of chardonnay, and a stack of our favorite magazines.

Of course, even on a snow day, we can't help the fact that our students are still on our hearts and our classrooms and lessons are on our minds. So sure, we'll give you plenty of unique classroom ideas and solutions, but we also want to offer what the professional development-centered publications don't.

Let's talk outfits, home, classroom design, one-handed copy machine snacks, and side hobbies. Let's take time for self care, look at the big picture, and expand into other valued priorities.

This magazine is for allowing yourself the time, mental space, and inspiration you need each quarter to get back to the basics. We blend teacher life with all the other beautiful dimensions of our lives.

It has been quite a journey to start building this for you, and I have never enjoyed any project so much. Every day that I sit down to work on this magazine, I feel so energized by the concept. I hope that each page brings you the same level of joy that I feel when I create it.

Let's dive into the fun stuff that makes us who we are! This magazine is for your Thursday evening bathtub soak, your summer vacation beach reading, your thrown-in-the-bag car reading for the wait time after your kids' sports practice, and your evening moment of peace with a cocktail on the patio.

Let Snowday be your guide to a productive, thoughtful, passionate life as an educator AND as a creative, vibrant human soul!

- Brigid

SPOTLIGHT THEMES IN THIS ISSUE: FOCUS, FUEL, & FOLIAGE

# FOCUS

What you focus on will increase, grow, or improve.

Throughout this issue, consider what you are focusing on in the broad scheme of your life. What are your priorities right now in your family, your classroom, and your personal life?

We also explore a narrower definition of "focus." How can you improve your students' attention in class? We share science-based ways to boost the focus of your class through creative approaches and by incorporating greenery.

Conscious Living >> 64
Productivity for Females >> 56
Creativity & the Brain >> 28
Focus on Feedback >> 8
Make the Most of Prep Time >> 72

# FUEL

Fuel your body; fuel your soul. It's time to chat about creative hobbies and endeavors that inspire you and fill you up as a human. When you are self-fulfilled, you can offer your best to your class and family.

As far as this issue is concerned, "fueling up" tips include coffee hacks, infused water recipes, setting aside time to recharge, and even filling up your retirement account!

Don't miss the "What will fuel your soul next?" worksheet. It's worth your time and will give you some surprising insights.

Coffee with Healthy Spice >> 74
Hydrating: Infused Water >> 80
Fuel Your Soul >> 110
Soul Inspiration >> 106, 108
Wealth for Teachers >> 36

# FOLIAGE

You may be surprised to discover what plants can do for your home and school.

We've got photos from teachers using plants to create atmosphere, filter the air, support learning, and even offer relaxation.

Get the facts about the benefits of foliage in work and school environments, then use our handy reference cards to help you and your students to keep the classroom plants healthy and happy. We've carefully chosen plant options for youngsters and newbies.

Plants in the Classroom >> 12, 20
Reference Cards - Plant Care >> 14
Air Plants >> 24
Permaculture >> 42

*You can do what I cannot do. I can do what you cannot do. Together we can do great things.*
>> Mother Teresa

**Editor & Publisher**
Brigid Danziger

**Editing & Proofreading**
Michael Dober

**Writers**
Kelly Barendt
Brigid Danziger
Carmen Myer

**Media Support**
Mike Bedell

**Sponsored and Produced by**
Math Giraffe, LLC

**Follow On Instagram**
@snowdaymagazine

**Contact Us**
editor@snowdaymagazine.com

**Advertising**
media@snowdaymagazine.com

**Website**
SNOWDAYMAGAZINE.COM

Copyright 2019

All rights reserved. Views, comments, and suggestions do not necessarily represent those of the publisher, and are provided as is. Snowday's editor and publisher disclaim any and all legal responsibility for the reader's use of any information included in this publication. Content given is not intended as a replacement for consulting an expert.

No portion of this publication may be reproduced without permission.

Cover images: Megan Rowe, twenty20

# BELL WORK

Is your classroom the one that gets the most noise complaints in your hall? Do you have students suffering from daily headaches from the flourescent lights? Do you lose your students' focus for an hour after lunch?

You'll be amazed at the way these small tweaks can transform your environment and lead to higher productivity, more relaxed focus time, and healthier bodies, minds, and attitudes!

### Objective:
Incorporate the five senses to create a more relaxing and inspiring classroom environment. Increase focus and activate learning by making small changes.

**1. VISUAL:**
Fluorescent lights can cause stress and headaches. If you cannot change your lighting, at least add a lamp or two to give other lighting options (Use natural daylight or warm toned bulbs).

**2. AUDITORY:**
Encourage collaborative, productive noise without having a loud, echoing room. Add aural "comfort" with fabric that absorbs sound. Try curtains, rugs, or throw pillows.

**3. TACTILE:**
Put out rubix cubes, or create a jigsaw puzzle corner to keep active fingers busy.

**4. SCENT:**
Try a flameless wax burner behind your desk. Scents like lavender, jasmine, and frankincense are calming, while switching out your wax for a rosemary or citrus scent is energizing and helps increase focus. Check any oils or waxes for child safety first.

**5. TASTE:**
Refill a jar of mints to offer an energy boost and help students pay attention.

# 5 FEEDBACK LANGUAGES

CUSTOMIZE HOW YOU COMMUNICATE TO HELP EVERY STUDENT HEAR WHAT YOU'RE REALLY TRYING TO SAY

One student in your class may be desperately wishing that you would just squat down in front of his desk, look him in the eye, and say "I am so proud of your work on that. I noticed how hard you tried after our last conversation." Another student who generally dreads one-on-one conversation would be completely uncomfortable if you did that, but would just light up inside to see a little note stuck on a completed worksheet showing that you noticed his effort and took time to write by hand what you thought of his work. He'd leave it attached in his homework folder and glow with pride when his parents open it up to read your words.

You may be familiar with the *5 Love Languages*, a #1 New York Times bestseller by Dr. Gary Chapman, where "Everyone gives and receives love differently, but with a little insight into these differences, we can be confidently equipped to communicate love well."

The 5 love languages encourage us to understand how our partners or friends give and receive love, so that we can effectively communicate and grow our relationships.

Knowing how the other person desires to receive attention or affection can help your relationship with your spouse or significant other, your friends, your family, and even your co-workers. But what about your relationships with your students? Well, we've created the equivalent of the five love languages for teachers!

# Give Students the Right Style & Fit of Feedback

You've heard of the 5 love languages, but now we are applying this idea to student needs. Each student has their own way to receive praise, feel receptive to a lecture, and connect with the important things you need to tell him/her as an individual.

*by Kelly Barendt*

Feedback in the classroom is a powerful tool that has the ability to make or break a child's school experience. You've likely already noticed that students have their own individual preferences on the way they receive feedback from their teachers. Some like positive feedback shouted out in front of the entire class, others prefer to talk to you one-on-one, and others appreciate when you notify their parents of their success.

Each student has a natural tendency to receive your "love" or feedback differently, just as people do in their relationships. You can grow your student-teacher relationships and make your students feel acknowledged and loved by determining their feedback language and using it.

As an added bonus, they'll be much more receptive to the feedback itself and focus on **what** you said if you truly know **how** they need it delivered.

Here are our 5 Feedback languages:

### 1. Silent Stamps of Approval
Some students prefer positive feedback to be directed to them in a silent, discreet way. They don't like being the center of attention, so drawing any sort of recognition their way can make them uncomfortable. To avoid this, implement one of our "Silent Stamps" to discreetly show them you recognize their success and are proud. Leave a handwritten note on the top of a graded assignment. Use stickers or stamps when grading. Leave a note for your student in his/her locker or desk when you notice positive behavior or attributes.

### 2. Shout It Out
On the flip side, some students love being the center of attention, even if just for a moment. They are filled with pride when their peers are made aware of their success. To affirm them in front of their peers, use more of the "Shout It Out" language. Tell the entire class when they do well on an assignment. Read their paper aloud, and get whole-group feedback.

### 3. Report Home
Reporting home means a lot to these students. It can be as simple as a quick email or text to their mom, dad, or other guardian notifying them of positive feedback. Or, if you have time, making a phone call home can mean even more. Parents' approval and pride in their child's achievements is so important to this child or teen's sense of self-worth.

### 4. Focused Attention
This language requires your undivided attention. Students who appreciate this language thrive when you get down on their level, make direct eye-contact, and give verbal feedback one-on-one. Taking a minute out of your day for giving quality time and feedback to a student can be worthwhile. Some students (like some teen males) may prefer side-by-side over direct eye contact.

### 5. Public Posting
These students love when others know about their achievements, but don't necessarily want it shouted out in class, or to have everyone's eyes on them. Talk to them in person to ask if it's ok if you post their work to the classroom's online page or share it in a schoolwide show. They won't have to be the center of attention, but can have the satisfaction of external views.

*make copies*

## What's Your Feedback Language?

# QUIZ

Circle the answer that best fits.

**1. If you do a great job on a test, you'd want your teacher to…**

a) Give you a sticker on your paper without saying anything.
b) Announce it to the whole class.
c) Call your parents with the news.
d) Call you over and tell you.
e) Share it on a class website.

**2. You finally get that math problem you've been trying to solve, You're going to tell…**

a) Nobody. You would rather keep it to yourself.
b) EVERYONE sitting around you!
c) Your parents.
d) Your teacher.
e) Online friends by posting on social media

**3. You screwed up and now you need a lecture or consequence. Which will make you straighten up and fly right? (be honest!)**

a) a written agreement to sign
b) an embarrassing moment where you are called out on your mistake
c) your teacher getting your parents involved
d) a heart to heart talk about the mistake with your teacher
e) losing your internet access for a week

**4. Who is your biggest motivator in school?**

a) Yourself
b) Your classmates
c) Your parents
d) Your teacher
e) The world outside your classroom

**5. You get an A+ on a writing assignment. Which reaction are you most excited for?**

a) Your internal proud feeling
b) Your classmates' reactions
c) Your parents' grins
d) Your teacher's praise
e) The "likes" you get on the internet

**6. Your teacher catches you doing a good deed. What do you do?**

a) Keep it to yourself.
b) Tell everyone around you!
c) Text mom or dad right away.
d) Feel proud and glad your teacher noticed.
e) Ask to be nominated for an award

If you got…

**Mostly a's**
Then your feedback language is Silent Stamp of Approval. You don't like being the center of attention, so you love when your teacher simply writes notes or adds stickers to your graded papers.

**Mostly b's**
Then your feedback language is Shout It Out. You like when your teacher announces your success to the whole class. Being the center of attention doesn't bother you.

**Mostly c's**
Then your feedback language is Report Home. Your parents' opinion matters the most to you. You love when your teacher tells your parents about your achievements.

**Mostly d's**
Then your feedback language is Focused Attention. You like when you feel respected by your teacher and when he/she talks to you privately and directly to give you feedback.

**Mostly e's**
Then your feedback language is Public Posting. You love when your good work is posted online or in a public place for everyone to see.

# FIND their FEEDBACK LANGUAGES

Now, you're probably wondering how to implement this with so many students. With this in mind, we created a short quiz that you can copy and give to your students. They'll answer the questions, and score their answers, giving you the data necessary to be aware of each student's feedback language!

# USE their FEEDBACK LANGUAGES

Just like the 5 Love Languages, it's important to remember that just because you know a student has a primary feedback language, you shouldn't neglect the other four. They are all important to a student's success and sense of self-worth, they just might be most receptive to one in particular.

## WHAT WOULD MEAN A LOT TO THIS STUDENT?

| Silent Stamp | Shout It Out | Report Home | Focused Attention | Public Posting |
|---|---|---|---|---|
| a simple sticky note | being used as an example | an email sharing details | scheduling a personalized one-on-one meeting | submission to a contest |
| a handwritten set of positive and negative feedback | being featured as a volunteer | an invitation for grandparents to come see a special presentation | sitting down beside him/her to talk | invitation to a club or group |
| a special, meaningful, or funny sticker | being mentioned aloud in small groups | | getting down to table level | feature on a web page or newsletter |
| a high five | being shown off in a whole-class setting | a phone call or text to the home | working together on the same paper | shoutout or public award |
| a silent thumbs up | having work on a bulletin board or hallway display | a note in the take-home folder | eye contact with hand on the shoulder | publication in a magazine, yearbook, art show, or online |
| a quiet little knowing nod | | a short home visit | | |

SNOWDAYMAGAZINE.COM | 11

# Plants in the Classroom

## Benefits of Having Plants in Class

Plants help regulate humidity to keep us comfortable. They also provide a mental and emotional boost. Seeing nature helps calm our minds and relax our bodies.

Having indoor plants is linked to positivity and health. Having plants in hospital rooms has been shown to speed recovery and boost spirits. A plant beside your bed will lower your heart rate as you rest and promote healthier sleep.

Studies have shown that plants in offices reduce illnesses by up to 60%! This definitely makes it worth a try during flu season.

NASA has proven that plants can even help clean the air by removing toxins.

Greenery also helps increase focus. Students in one study were up to 70% more attentive in rooms with houseplants.

## Tips for Success:

Place one plant in your classroom for each 120 square feet.

Try to have one visible from each viewpoint in the room for optimal mental health impact.

Succulents are a good start if you want to ease in. They are smaller, but very easy to care for. Aloe is a great plant for a first attempt.

Let your students choose silly names for the plants if they wish. They will take great pride in caring for the life they are nurturing in their classroom.

Make plant care a classroom job. Let your classroom gardener use these reference cards on the following pages for tips on water, sunlight, and drainage.

We've organized some of the best plants into categories, so you can select the ones that best fit your classroom needs.

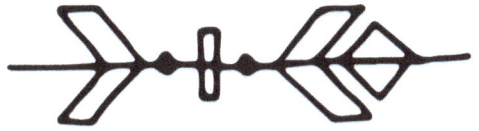

# Easy-Care Favorites

Try these plants for an easy start. Laminate these cards for student reference. Put them onto bamboo skewers or stakes to keep them in each pot.

## Dracaena

**Water:**
Mist the leaves with water, and water until the drainage holes drip, but not very often. The soil should never be soggy. Be sure the soil is very dry (a whole finger deep without feeling any moisture) before watering.

**Sunlight:**
Place away from windows.

**Care Tips:**
If lower leaves yellow and fall off, that is fine, but if other leaves yellow, it means it's overwatered.

## Snake Plant
*Sansevieria*

**Water:**
Allow soil to dry between waterings. Do not over-water, especially in winter. Once every couple of weeks is usually enough. Avoid getting the leaves wet.

**Sunlight:**
Place in indirect light (in sunny area but not right in the window.)

**Care Tips:**
Fertilize during the growing season.

## Money Tree
*Pachira Aquatica*

**Water:**
Allow soil to dry between waterings. Watering once a week is usually enough. If the soil seems soggy, do not water.

**Sunlight:**
Place it a few feet away from the window. It can even handle a bit of shade.

**Care Tips:**
Fertilize quarterly.

Fun Fact: The dracaena is from the asparagus family! It helps improve air quality.

### Bonsai
Dwarf Juniper

**Water:**
Water moderately. Check the soil by pressing your finger in to see if the top layer is all dry. If the top half inch is dry, it needs water.

**Sunlight:**
Place in morning sunlight, but do not let it get too much direct sun in the heat of the day.

**Care Tips:**
Fertilize during growing months. Prune in the spring, and repot every year or two.

Try these plants if your students are older, or you have more experience with plants. These are more sensitive to temperature changes and need more care, such as fertilizing, pruning, or repotting.

You'll want to supplement these basic care cards with additional tips online, and even seek out tutorial videos.

### Bird of Paradise

**Water:**
Water regularly. Be sure it is not too wet, but don't let the soil dry out completely. Periodically, water it more deeply, giving it a good soak every couple weeks in the hotter months. Let it dry out just a bit more in the darker winter months.

**Sunlight:**
Place in full, direct sunlight. Rotate each week so that all sides get plenty of light.

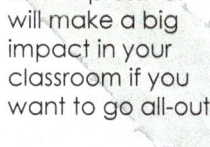

The bird of paradise is large and impressive. It will make a big impact in your classroom if you want to go all-out!

# More Ambitious Options

# Full-Size Plants

These options will work if you have a large empty space. These are potted trees, so be sure you have plenty of floor space in the room, and an appropriate sunlight situation.

Like with any plant, be sure that you have the correct soil type. Layer your potting plan to account for drainage. This means you will want a plastic drip tray under the plastic pot with holes. Set the entire package inside of an attractive pot, basket, or bowl in the classroom.

Remind students to check the drainage tray when they water to avoid overflowing. Keep a few gallon jugs on hand in your classroom. Students can water without a sink nearby, and only have to refill the bottles from the restroom sinks every few weeks.

## Rubber Plant
### Ficus Elastica

**Water:**
Give it plenty of water during the growing season. Wipe leaves periodically with a damp cloth. Only water once a month during dormant season.

**Sunlight:**
Give it bright light, but don't let it get too hot. A window with sheer curtains is perfect.

**Care Tips:**
Yellow leaves will show that the plant is getting too much water.

## Fiddle Leaf Fig

**Water:**
Allow soil to dry between waterings. Then soak it until water runs out of drainage holes.

**Sunlight:**
Place in a nice sunny window for penty of light. Avoid drafts. Move it away if the window is open. Turn it if it starts leaning toward the light.

**Care Tips:**
If new leaves turn brown and drop off, it needs more water. If lower leaves brown and drop, it needs less water. Fertilize during growth season.

## Spider Plant
### Chlorophytum Comosum

**Water:**
Water frequently, but do not allow soil to remain soggy.

**Sunlight:**
Place in bright, but indirect light in a cool room.

**Care Tips:**
Prune by cutting the plant back down to its base.

Browning is normal. Try giving the plant a deep watering to rinse out any extra salt content in the soil.

## Hoya Carnosa

**Water:**
Do not overwater. Wait until the leaves look a little bit "puckered."

**Sunlight:**
Place in medium indirect light, a bit away from the sunny window.

**Care Tips:**
Fertilize in the spring and summer.

Don't cut back the tendrils. This is where flowers will form in a healthy plant.

Short on free surfaces? If you do not have any floor space, windowsill space, or table space to spare, you can still give classroom plants a try! These hanging options help make plant life accessible in even the most packed spaces.

# Hanging Plants

## for the little ones

### Tips for plant care with younger students

If you don't have a classroom sink, fill a gallon jug once a week. Students (or you) can fill a cup with a spout for watering as needed without having to hike down the hall to the restroom.

Purchase see-through toddler cups that are NOT spill proof and draw a "fill line" so once the cup is filled, students can pour just the right amount into each plant pot at a nice slow pace and avoid spills.

Show little ones how to pull a new baby spider plant from the stem of a large spider plant. It's easy to see a new plant grow by placing the small one into a jar of water while you wait for the roots to grow. Once they do, transfer the baby plant into a new pot with soil.

Provide a mister and allow students to mist leaves and gently wipe dust off as a reward.

Avoid plant stands with tall legs. Place pots and drainage dishes directly on the floor, table, or windowsill. Stick to wider, heavy pots so they do not tip as little bodies scamper around the room.

# Flowering Beauties

Wishing for some color? These lovely floral options are still relatively easy to care for, and will brighten up your classroom space in a breeze!

These are best for classrooms with older students.

### Peace Lily
#### Spathiphyllum

**Water:**
Keep the soil moist, but do not overwater. Filtered water is a better option than tap water because the plant is sensitive to chemicals. Keep the humidity high, and mist as needed.

**Sunlight:**
Place in morning sunlight, but keep away from the strength of the mid-day harsher sunshine.

**Care Tips:**
This plant is poisonous if ingested. Keep away from young children and animals. Repot in fresh soil annually.

### African Violet

**Water:**
Let water sit out overnight, then gently use the lukewarm water to water the soil only. Do not let the plant itself get wet. Water frequently enough that soil is always moist, but never puddled.

**Sunlight:**
Place in strong, but filtered light.

**Care Tips:**
Pinch off dead flowers, and fertilize if flowering decreases.

**Added Bonus:**

With flowering plants, if you have enough blooms (or plenty of separate plants), you can allow one student to cut a small bouquet each week to take home to a mother, sister, or other caregiver. This will make their day! You can make it a reward, or just choose a student who seems to need a little pick-me-up each week.

Nathan van der Monde's 6th grade classroom has an abundance of greenery.

"Having plants and greenery in the classroom learning space is vital for so many reasons. It is visually appealing and stimulating, the plants themselves are releasing oxygen into the air keeping our brains working at optimum levels, and they create a naturally calm ambience that improves students' work output and we're all the happier for it!"

>> Nathan van der Monde
@mrvandermonde

Do you have plants in your classroom?

*call a plant beautiful and it becomes a flower. call it ugly and it becomes a weed >> jonathan lockwood huie*

Nikki, a 4th year elementary and middle school art teacher, added some fun succulents to the windowsill of her art room.

Shared by @lopatcongart

These class plants are cared for by student waterers, who are doing a great job! The plants are named Diablo, Neo & Ms. Eng.

shared by Christal @christalintentions

"My classroom is slowly becoming an indoor garden and I'm LOVING it!! My students help me take care of all these lovely plants. They water them, pick the dead leaves, etc. It's been such a fun addition to my small office space!"

Shared by Trish, special ed teacher @dueverdesigns

I love the cute teacher things as much as everyone else but... I have told myself it is all unnecessary and in turn decided to buy classroom plants every time I feel the need for more cute classroom plastic junk. Plants are such a great addition to classrooms and kids love to take care of them. And the string of pearls are fake because I love them and kill them every year.

For some teacher self care I got my sansevieria family new pots and stand! Most my classroom is sansevieria plants because they are so durable and hard to kill! I wish I could put so many more plants in the classroom! I use the same Ikea pots in my classroom as well.

Shared by @craftandteach

# All About Air Plants

*the new trend in houseplants*

*my fake plants died because i did not pretend to water them >> mitch hedberg*

Air plants used to be rare, but now they are becoming available as experts propagate more and more types. There are now more than 650 varieties available, and you can probably find them at your local nursery. These fun new plants are trendy for a reason. They're incredibly easy to take care of.

They do not even need to be planted! Air plants just require air circulation, and occasional watering. Often, in nature, they attach themselves to rocks or other plants.

Air plants have a tendency to "latch on" to rocks, trees, or other surfaces. Make a fun display by attaching them, grouping them, or creating a little terrarium that kids can re-arrange.

These may be a perfect fit for your home or classroom because they are so low maintenance.

## Selecting your air plants

Choose an air plant with a silvery hue if you'd like it to be drought tolerant. A plant with more of a green tint will require you to pay more attention to water needs. The greener the plant, the more quickly it will dry out.

## Watering your air plants

Most air plants will need to be watered about once a week, but some can go up to two weeks before needing a rinse. To water them, just run them under the faucet with gentle water pressure. Set them in the sink to drain. Once they are not dripping, you can place them back in their containers.

Misting them with a spray bottle, or leaving them in a moist environment (like your shower) can also help keep the humidity level high for the plants.

If the base of the plant does dry out a bit, just remove the dried foliage and give it a nice long soak in a container of water.

## Keeping your air plants warm

For best results, keep your plants in a warm area, away from direct sunlight. If your plant is extra happy with its conditions, it will reward you for such good care by flowering and generating new baby plants from the original!

## Surrounding your air plants with beauty

>> Try a glass terarrium with a bit of gravel.

>> Hang it in a pretty hanging planter.

>> Try a grid of them on a wall in small cups.

>> Snuggle them up against a mossy plant that holds water to keep them moist.

>> Do not use soil.

>> Add fun decorative touches in the terrarium for a tiny garden vibe.

>> You can use fishing wire, or even a bit of hot glue to gently attach them to other items, hang them, group them, or mount them on a display!

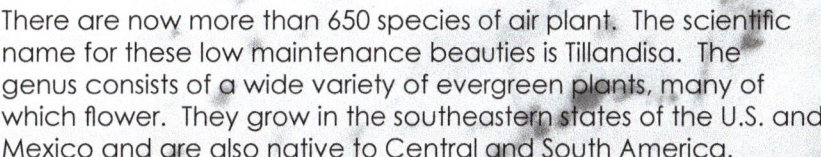

*rinse*

There are now more than 650 species of air plant. The scientific name for these low maintenance beauties is Tillandisa. The genus consists of a wide variety of evergreen plants, many of which flower. They grow in the southeastern states of the U.S. and Mexico and are also native to Central and South America.

Most of the nutrients that an air plant needs can be absorbed from the air surrounding them. When you first purchase or receive an air plant, give it a long soak. It will need this periodically. Let it sit in water for 20-45 minutes, then allow it to dry out for a day or so by sitting out on a paper towel (preferably upside-down).

Its water needs will shift with the seasons. When the weather is hot or dry, mist it often, and give it a rinse or even a soak more frequently. When the weather is chilly, it may not need much other than the air around it.

As your air plant grows, it may need more soaking. A baby plant may be happy with just a gentle mist here and there, or a humid room. Middle school students add plenty of (odiferous) humidity, as we know! Assess the moisture level of your classroom or home, and give water accordingly.

Air plants are flexible in their needs. Soak your plant every few weeks when you think of it, and don't worry if you put it in water as you prep your lesson plans for the next day at 3:30, and then accidentally leave it overnight. It will be fine with an overnight soak here and there. The key is to be sure that it dries out before you place it back in its container. You will want to avoid putting it back in its habitat while it is wet, as that can cause mold.

Tighter curls on the leaves will show you that the plant needs a bit more moisture. Keep the indirect sunlight coming, and offer plenty of air circulation, and your air babies should survive well, and even thrive!

*soak*

*mist*

*you only need one*

Plants will grow and then bloom to reproduce. When you see your air plant grow "pups" from its base, leave them alone a while. Once they are close to half the size of the parent plant, you can separate them and have new plants!

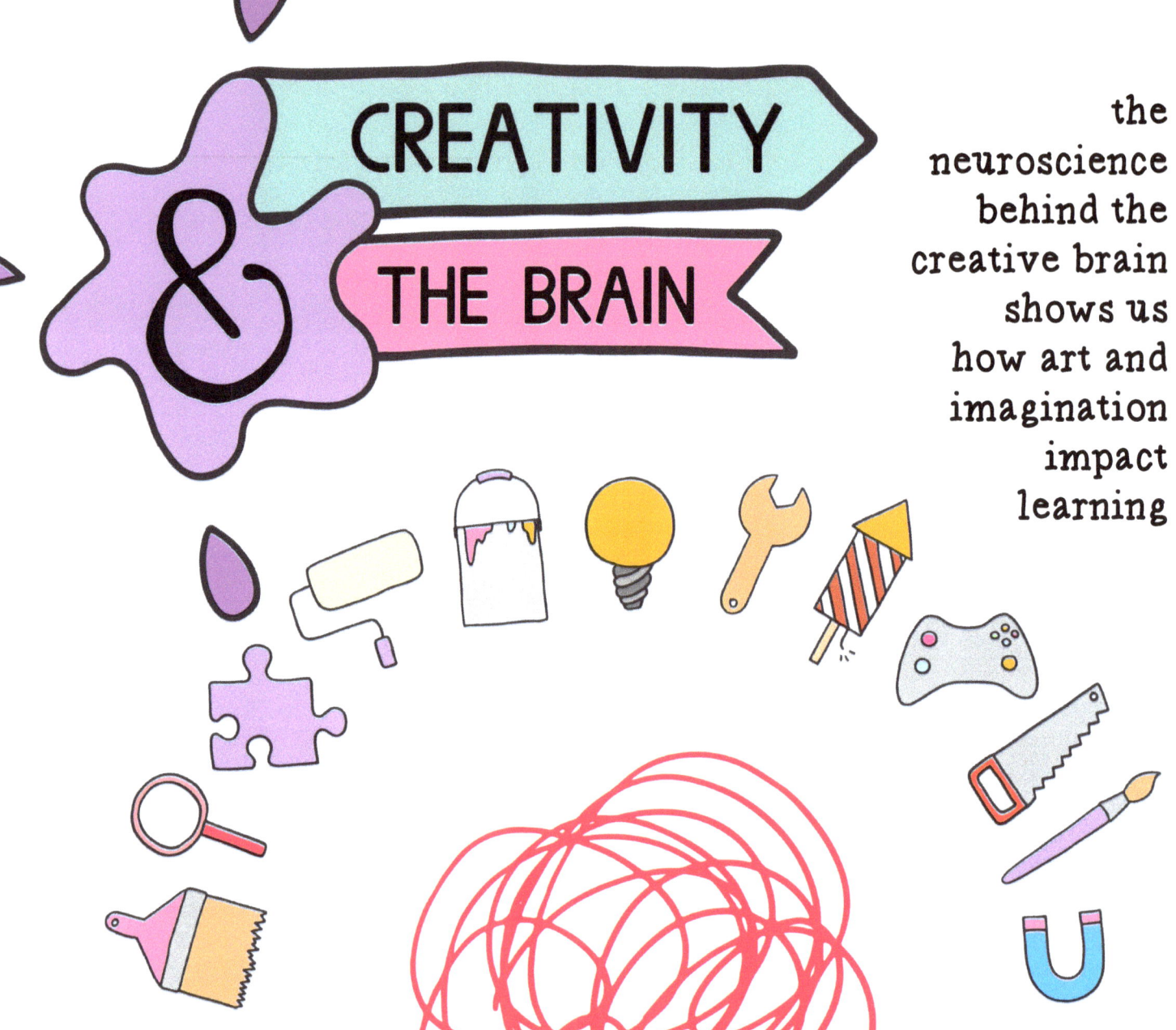

# CREATIVITY & THE BRAIN

the neuroscience behind the creative brain shows us how art and imagination impact learning

Is it true that certain people are just inherently creative? Are some of us born with creative minds and others just lack that innovative touch? It turns out that all minds are designed for creativity. Once we know how to nurture the creative mind, we can harness its full potential, both in the classroom and beyond.

Creativity is thought to come mostly from the subconscious mind. It may be true that some people have a more natural ability to "tap" into that inventive layer, but that doesn't mean that the others do not have it.

**Creativity is for All Brains**
According to an article from Forbes, (Study Reveals How Creative Brains are Wired), a new study reveals that people who are being "creative" with ideas can do so when they are able to incorporate different neural networks within the brain to work together. By engaging three main networks in the brain that don't always cooperate, some people were able to generate more creative ideas than others. The researchers discovered that creativity doesn't simply come from the left or right side of the brain; "it is a whole-brain endeavor."

Creativity is not something that some people have and some do not. We need to encourage both hemispheres and a variety of mental systems within the brain to work together to really maximize the benefits of creativity.

What exactly does it mean to have these types

of neuroconnections? Early psychologist and researcher, Frank X. Barron decided to try to tackle these questions in a historical study at the University of California - Berkeley campus. Here were some of his findings:

>> IQ alone could not explain the creative spark.
>> Creativity uses a host of intellectual, emotional, motivational and moral characteristics.
>> Brains working creatively have a preference for complexity and ambiguity.
>> Creative genius requires a high tolerance for disorder and disarray.
>> Innovative minds have the ability to extract order from chaos.
>> A willingness to take risks goes a long way toward creative thinking.

Barron realized that creative brains had a mixed blend of traits, "both more primitive and more cultured, more destructive and more constructive, occasionally crazier and yet adamantly saner, than the average person."

So, what is the neuroscience behind this creative brain, and how can we achieve this creative genius for our own minds?

diffused thinking occurs when the mind is allowed to WANDER... daydream... imagine...
- Barbara Oakley

There are many facets to creativity, and that's why it is a process that utilizes the entire brain. Another psychologist, Mihaly Csikszentmihalyi, spent more than 3 decades studying creatives. He concluded "If I had to express in one word what makes their personalities different from others, it's complexity. They show tendencies of thought and action that in most people are segregated. They contain contradictory extremes; instead of being an 'individual,' each of them is a 'multitude.'"

Different neural networks are activated when certain tasks are being completed. However, a more creative brain accesses each one a little differently, and blends thought processes that do not always meld naturally. The three large scale neural networks that must interact for visionary thought to occur are the executive attention network, the imagination network, and the salience network.

**The Large Scale Neural Networks:**
The first of the three brain networks involved in creative thinking is called the "Executive Attention Network." Since it's recruited when the brain requires attention that is highly focused, this network is most likely active when concentrating on complex problem solving, listening to a challenging lecture, or engaging in heavy reasoning.

The second, the "Imagination Network," also called the "Default Network," is involved in using personal past experiences to create mental simulations, think about the future, and imagine possible scenarios that occur in daily life. Also, it is used in social cognition when we're trying to assess what someone else is thinking.

The "Salience Network" is the last. We need to constantly monitor the external events of our lives with our steady internal stream of consciousness. Depending on what information is the most salient to solving the task at hand, the salience network takes the reins.

These three critical neural networks need to interact smoothly to foster creative thinking. This was reflected in recent research on jazz musicians and their ability to create such wondrous improvisational music. It's what neuroscientists like to call a flow state.

Of course this is just a tip of the iceberg when it comes to understanding the depth of our creative cognitive abilities. It's still good to know that our creativity has better roots than just one side of our brain. It takes both sides of brain, working together in networks to have creative thought. The innovations we acheive from this whole-brain collaboration can not only help us create literature and art, but it can also be used to come up with creative solutions to problems.

Creative thinking has led us to the most fundamental discoveries in geometry, physics, and more. This ability to problem solve and innovate is vital to our students' future success.

We should not hesitate to teach all of our subjects, even math and literature, more creatively to allow students to tap into the different levels of thinking.

**Left Brain vs. Right Brain**
When we think about how the brain works, we often think about the hemispheres. One of the first questions that comes to mind is, "Are you left-brained or right-brained?" In fact, just searching the term on the internet will give you an onslaught of personality tests to learn your "predominant hemisphere."

The theory is that you must know if you use your brain mostly through an artsy, imaginative drive or through analytical, logical reasoning. Once you know whether you are left-brained or right-brained, you'll be able to know how to learn better, teach better, and harness your cognition, right?

Actually, not quite. However popular this train of thought is, it is not entirely accurate.

More than 1,000 brains went under analysis at the University of Utah and they found no evidence to support this idea that people are left- or right- brained. The results showed that all of the participants were using their entire brain equally, concluding that our left brain-right brain ideas are mostly just a myth. This shows that creative brains aren't just housed in the right side of our cranium. There's so much more that happens to us when our brains are ignited with creativity.

The right and left hemispheres of the brain communicate through the corpus callosum, a fiber bridge that crosses between the two sides. Crossing the corpus callosum engages the full brain to increase focus, memory, creativity, problem solving skills, and more.

**Teaching with Creativity**
Creativity does not tend to take center stage in many typical core subject classrooms, although it has been proven to have many benefits. According to The Lab School, "the educational community largely embraces the notion that creative expression is an important aspect of a student's learning experience. We also know that exposure to the arts and arts-integrated instruction has positive educational benefits, especially for learners who have not succeeded in typical

executive

PROBLEM SOLVING, FOCUSING ON THE TASK AT HAND

REMEMBERING, THINKING ABOUT THE FUTURE, VISUALIZING ALTERNATE SCENARIOS

imagination

salience

AWARENESS OF OUTSIDE STIMULI AND INTERNAL CONSCIOUSNESS, CONTROLLING SWITCHES AND SHIFTS BETWEEN NETWORKS

Make an empty space in any corner of your mind, and creativity will instantly fill it. >> Dee Hock

**Creative thinking skills**

HELP DEVELOP INTRINSIC MOTIVATION

HELP STUDENTS BECOME LIFELONG LEARNERS.

learning environments."

Creative thinking skills help develop intrinsic motivation and help students become lifelong learners. Children and teens must be given the opportunity to seek out new experiences and experiment with new ideas. They should be taught to ask questions and investigate to help develop critical thinking and problem solving skills. Art, innovation, and creation help to encourage this.

In addition to all of the brain-based benefits, creative expression offers the added bonus of fun and relaxation. Students love to have the opportunity to relax and use their creative sides. School days can be monotonous if there are no opportunities for different areas of the brain to engage and activate.

The way the executive, imagination, and salience neural networks interact can help us understand creative cognition. They will activate and deactivate according to the needs of the task. So, if you're trying to create a painting it might be best to let your mind wander a bit. This means deactivating your Executive Network and letting your Imagination Network take center stage. Then once you have your ideas, you'll need to access your focus to take these ideas and bring them to reality. And the Salience Network helps us do exactly that.

This effect is similar to the effect that coloring, doodling, and sketching while learning a new math concept can offer. Strategies like visual note-taking, color coding, and mind mapping help students' brains to shift between these networks. Even incorporating activities that require music, color, noise, teamwork, or art will start to get these neural pathways engaged. We can activate neurons from each category to increase the brain's effectiveness and give student creativity a boost.

Science Daily shared a study from last year in which a team of researchers used fNIRS (functional near-infrared spectroscopy) to measure blood flow in the areas of the brain related to rewards while the study participants completed three different art activities: coloring in a mandala, doodling around or within a circle on paper, and free-drawing.

During these three-minute activities (with rests in between), researchers found an increase in blood flow in the prefrontal cortex of the brain.
According to this article, "the prefrontal cortex is related to regulating our thoughts, feelings and actions. It is also related to emotional and motivational systems and part of the wiring for our brain's reward circuit. So seeing increased bloodflow in these areas likely means a person is experiencing feelings related to being rewarded."

Embracing teaching strategies that incorporate all three neural networks will activate those positive emotions, relax students, and achieve better learning results.

### Igniting the Creative Spark

How can you get your students' creative juices flowing? How can you get your own creative mind inspired when you are working on a project yourself? How does a creative mind spark?

An article from Psychology Today (Get Some Headspace – How to Nurture Your Creativity) puts it this way, "The reason we are often unaware of creative, inspirational and spontaneous thoughts is generally because the surface of the mind is constantly moving. The busy-ness of the mind creates ripples on the surface, in just the same way as throwing a stone into a pond creates ripples on the surface of the water. The problem is, most people get so caught up in the appearance of these ripples that the water never has a chance to settle. Again, just imagine looking into a pool of water… The calmer the water, the clearer the reflection.

Again, the mind is no different, when the surface-thinking settles, it becomes much easier to see the contents of the mind – and therefore become conscious of the creative thoughts which you were previously not conscious of!"

**Diffused Thinking**
There is a difference between focused thinking and diffused thinking.

Barbara Oakley, professor and author of Learning How to Learn, teaches that "Diffused thinking occurs when you allow your mind to wander, to imagine and to daydream. In this mode, the brain is still working -- consolidating information and making sense of what you are trying to learn."

We use diffused thinking when we do things like go for a walk, ponder things in the shower, or doodle absentmindedly in a notebook.

This would easily explain why we seem to get "struck" with creative thoughts when we are having downtime like walking, taking a shower, or relaxing. This is because your mind is quiet. There aren't a lot of other thoughts cluttering your mind and blocking your creativity.

So, how do we nurture this creative side of our minds?

>> Do imagination exercises – Complete a creative challenge every day. It can be as simple as a game where you pick a random word and then a random medium. Then you have to create something using both of those parameters. For example, take a word like "flower" and then a medium like "pipe cleaners." Then see what you can make with the two ideas.

>> Take time for meditation and reflection – Meditation and creativity go hand in hand. Meditation helps to calm and clear your mind, allowing those creative thoughts to flow more easily. Your intuitive awareness is increased, and that helps you nurture your creative side.

>> Get plenty of sleep – A good night of rest ensures that your mind is running at full capacity the next day. You are less likely to get bogged down in thoughts because you will be sharper and more open to creative thoughts during the day.

>> Spend time with nature – Getting out in nature is one of the best ways to nurture the creative mind. A simple walk in the park or your neighborhood could be enough to harness your creative side.

>> Pursue hobbies and interest that energize you – Picking up a simple hobby that you've always wanted to try will help you enjoy some downtime. They don't necessarily have to have a goal or special outcome; but certain activities, like yoga or Tai Chi will help connect the body and mind. Whatever it is, you want to make sure to make time for yourself. This will improve your intuitive awareness, leaving you more creative than ever.

It is reassuring to know that we all have the ability to be wildly creative and imaginative. While some people have a more natural inclination to connect with creative thoughts, it's something that is inside all of us. With a little bit of practice and relaxation, anyone can tap into a more creative place.

So this week, practice creative thinking. When you need an imaginative solution to one of life's problems, switch gears and jump in the shower, enjoy a hobby, or take a nice walk.

Other Sources: Live Science, Psychology Today, Forbes

DIFFUSED THINKING ALLOWS THE MIND TO BECOME CONSCIOUS OF THE CREATIVE THOUGHTS THAT OTHERWISE WOULD TEND TO REMAIN UNCONSCIOUS, BURIED IN THE BRAIN.

UNUSED CREATIVITY IS
NOT BENIGN.

IT METASTASIZES.

IT TURNS INTO GRIEF,
RAGE, JUDGEMENT,
SORROW, SHAME.

WE ARE CREATIVE BEINGS.

WE ARE BY NATURE
CREATIVE.

&gt;&gt; BRENE BROWN &lt;&lt;

# Your Guide to Rug Types

**A.** The sisal plant is a type of agave, and provides stiff fibers up to three feet long that can form rope, twine, and rug material. A sisal rug will be rough, stiff, and scratchy, but is stronger and more durable than most other natural woven rugs. Over time, sisal can become more slippery underfoot, so avoid using it in stairways or bathrooms. Sisal rugs last well, but stains become absorbed quickly. Choose sisal for a high traffic area that primarily gets walked on, not used as seating or playspace, and it should outlive other natural options.

**B.** Jute fibers are long and soft, similar to flax or hemp. They can be spun into coarse, but strong threads that form rough fabrics such as burlap. Jute is more affordable than many other rug materials and will offer a surface that is thick, soft, and vacuum-friendly. However, it won't do well with moisture, and will absorb odors or liquids. Jute rugs can shed a bit. You may want to find one that is backed with a soft, cushioned fabric, as they can become quite comfortable! Jute is a cozy choice in a dry, food-free room.

**C.** Seagrass is an underwater flowering plant found in saltwater marshes, and not a "grass" at all! A seagrass rug is a healthy and sustainable option. The plant is quick-growing and easy to harvest. This eco-friendly material provides plenty of texture and is more stain-resistant than other natural options. Choose a seagrass rug for a low-maintenance, earthy appeal. It will be easy to clean and is an environmentally conscious selection.

**D.** Wool can be a pricier choice, because animals cost more in upkeep and harvesting than plants. But that price comes with some benefits. A wool rug will keep its shape and is somewhat stain-resistant. The soft comfort of wool will outlast the more temporary cushion of a synthetic rug. Wool is strong, fire-resistant, and sustainable. One of the only downsides to wool is that it will hold water, so it becomes prone to mildew in wet environments.

**E.** Synthetic fibers like nylon or polyester are petroleum products (plastic) and are less eco-friendly and potentially less safe. These materials will also break down more quickly, so the durability cannot compete with natural rug materials. However, they can be more stain-resistant and much lower in cost. A synthetic rug is often a comfortable option for a home or classroom.

*The perfect rug can transform your classroom or living room. Once you know whether your area requires durability, stain resistance, or comfort, you can select just the right fit.*

Ideas

&gt;&gt; Natural fiber rugs have a great texture for gripping the rubber circles that many teachers use as students' floor spots.

&gt;&gt; Give your home or classroom a fun, neutral vibe by stitching a few textured runners side by side to create a fun, sectioned larger rug.

&gt;&gt; You can mix and match as you hunt for deals, because most natural fibers are neutral in color. Your collection can easily look cohesive in the same room. Combine and layer them for a calming look.

&gt;&gt; For a space-saving option, find bath mats on clearance. These can be used as mobile mini-rugs that students can grab to create a cozy spot in the corner of the classroom.

# BUILDING wealth
## ON A TEACHER SALARY

by Kelly Barendt

*detailed insights for managing your finances from teacher retirement accounts to investment and budgeting options*

---

**In effect, teacher salaries are decreasing.**
The average American still would be shocked to realize that many teachers in the U.S. make less than $30,000 per year. The U.S. average public school teacher salary for 2016–17 was $59,660. State average teacher salaries ranged from those in New York ($81,902), California ($79,128), and Massachusetts ($78,100) at the high end, to Mississippi ($42,925), Oklahoma ($45,292) and West Virginia ($45,555) at the low end.

The U.S. average one-year change in public school teacher salaries from 2015–16 to 2016–17 was 2.0 percent. The largest one-year decrease was in West Virginia (-0.1%), and the largest one-year increase was in South Dakota (11.8%).

The average classroom teacher salary for 2017-18 is estimated to increase by 1.4 percent over 2016-17, from $59,660 to $60,483.

The estimated average teacher salary of $60,483 for 2017-18 represents an increase of 11.2 percent over $54,368 in 2008-09.
But, when the effects of inflation are taken into account, the **average classroom teacher salary has actually decreased by 4.0 percent** from 2008-09 to 2017-18.

*(Stats from NEA Rankings of States 2017 & Estimates of School Statistics 2018)*

It's a fair assumption that you didn't go into teaching for the money; you are most

 **40% OF AMERICANS CANNOT AFFORD AN UNEXPECTED $400 EXPENSE**

likely passionate about improving the lives of our future generations. You work before and after school hours, and have probably used some of your personal money to do your best to provide a special, valuable education for your students. When it comes down to it - you care. We need more people like you in the world.

Does that mean you should sacrifice a comfortable life or your right to retire with dignity? Absolutely not. We're going to lay out detailed insights from professionals for managing your finances, all customized specifically for teachers!

### Finance Tips for Teachers from a Pro

Dave Ramsey, the founder of Ramsey Solutions, helps individuals like yourself achieve financial peace. Ramsey Solutions uses common-sense education and empowerment that give HOPE to everyone in every walk of life. Dave provides insight on a better retirement plan for teachers.

### Saving for Retirement

In the past, teachers relied on state-run pension plans to provide most of their retirement income. Now, teacher pension plans are underfunded by billions of dollars, and states have been forced to cut benefits for future retirees.

According to Dave Ramsey, "teachers can no longer depend on their pensions to provide the same retirement lifestyle yesterday's teachers enjoyed. It's now more important than ever that teachers have a plan to supplement their pensions with their own savings."

The most common option for teachers to save for retirement is through a 403(b). It's similar to a 401K (for workers in the private sector); contributions are automatically deducted pre-tax from pay, and the money grows tax-deferred until it's withdrawn in retirement. These benefits are great, but the big downside is the investment options. The choices are often overloaded with insurance products like annuities and variable annuities that have low returns and expensive fees and surrender charges. At first glance, these options might seem like a good deal. Many protect teachers' principal so they don't lose the money they put in, and annuities guarantee an income for life at retirement. However, they can have high fees that eat teacher's savings, and low returns keep what's left from growing.

Mutual funds don't have a principal guarantee and come with more risk, but offer higher potential growth, and their fees aren't too high. However, 403(b)s usually offer an extremely limited choice of mutual funds.

Dave Ramsey established "Baby Steps" everyone should take to work toward retiring with dignity. These steps can also help teachers and improve situations with extremely limited choices of mutual funds.

**NEARLY HALF OF U.S. FAMILIES HAVE A TOTAL RETIREMENT SAVINGS OF**  **$0**

## EVEN $1 MILLION SAVED IS NOT ENOUGH FOR THE AVERAGE RETIREE TO CONTINUE PAYING THE BILLS THEY CURRENTLY HAVE

# teacher - friendly
# SIDE GIGS

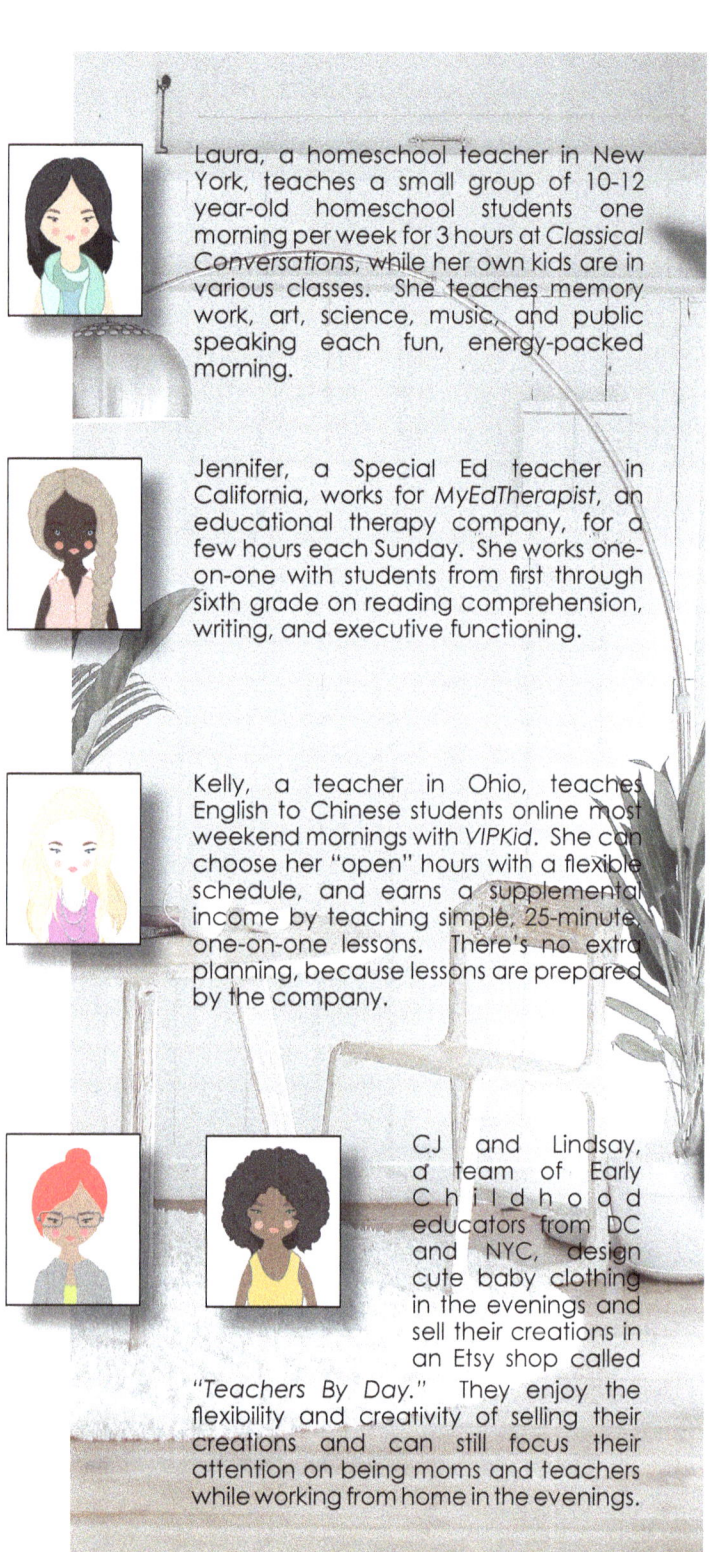

Laura, a homeschool teacher in New York, teaches a small group of 10-12 year-old homeschool students one morning per week for 3 hours at *Classical Conversations*, while her own kids are in various classes. She teaches memory work, art, science, music, and public speaking each fun, energy-packed morning.

Jennifer, a Special Ed teacher in California, works for *MyEdTherapist*, an educational therapy company, for a few hours each Sunday. She works one-on-one with students from first through sixth grade on reading comprehension, writing, and executive functioning.

Kelly, a teacher in Ohio, teaches English to Chinese students online most weekend mornings with *VIPKid*. She can choose her "open" hours with a flexible schedule, and earns a supplemental income by teaching simple, 25-minute, one-on-one lessons. There's no extra planning, because lessons are prepared by the company.

CJ and Lindsay, a team of Early Childhood educators from DC and NYC, design cute baby clothing in the evenings and sell their creations in an Etsy shop called *"Teachers By Day."* They enjoy the flexibility and creativity of selling their creations and can still focus their attention on being moms and teachers while working from home in the evenings.

*creative ways to make ends meet when the budget still falls short*

**Dave Ramsey's Baby Steps:**
>> After starting a small emergency fund, get out of debt.

>> Save up a full emergency fund that will cover 3-6 months of expenses.

>> Set a goal to invest 15% of your income for retirement.

>> Once you have that stability, you can save for college, pay off your home, build additional wealth, and be generous with any extra.

When you're ready to start investing, you'll need to divide that 15% in a way that works for you, depending on whether you get a "match" on the money you put in.

**If You Receive a Matching Contribution**
If your school system matches contributions to your 403(b), contribute enough to receive the match and choose the best mutual fund options included in your plan. Even if the funds aren't the best, you don't want to turn down a 100% return on your money.

Invest the remainder of your 15% in a Roth IRA. Roth IRAs allow your savings to grow tax-free, and you won't have to pay taxes on the money you withdraw when you retire. You can also choose from thousands of mutual fund options.
Select good, growth stock mutual funds in each of these categories: growth, aggressive growth, growth and income, and international. You could invest up to $5,500 in a Roth IRA in 2014.

**Don't Get a Match? No Problem**
If you don't receive a match in your 403(b), start by investing in a Roth IRA up to the limit. If you max out your Roth and have money left over, invest that portion in your 403(b) to take advantage of the tax-deferred growth.

For teachers who are required to contribute to their school retirement plan, Dave recommends you also invest in a Roth IRA. There are lots of variables here, so talk this over with your investing advisor to make sure you're saving enough to supplement your pension—or even replace it if your state's plan goes belly-up.

And if you leave your school district for a new job, roll your savings into an IRA so you have more investment options and the opportunity for higher returns on your investments.

**What if you're eligible to contribute to a 457(b)?**
Some public school teachers may be eligible to

**TOTAL MEDIAN RETIREMENT SAVINGS**

for 32-37 year old Americans in 2013

contribute to a 457(b). There are many similarities to a 403(b) plan, but also some key differences, like a 10% penalty if you withdraw prior to 59 ½ years of age from a 403(b) versus no penalty if you withdraw early from a 457(b).

Usually the 457(b) has a better structure, but Podcasters Dan Otter and Scott Dauenhauer from Teach and Retire Rich, strongly advise you don't make assumptions and choose a 457(b) over a 403(b). If you are trying to decide between the two plans, listen to episode #63, The 457(b) Plan from their podcast.

There's also a possibility that you are able to contribute to both your 403(b) and 457(b) plan. Many people don't know that if you contribute to both, your contributions to one doesn't affect the limit to the other, so you can contribute a substantial amount of income.

The teacher retirement system is definitely complex, and can seem mind-boggling at times, but remember that you do not have to make these decisions without helpful advice from experts.

You can also consider getting help from a fiduciary advisor at 403(b)wise. All of the advisors are Certified Financial Planners and signed a Fiduciary pledge, meaning they are obligated to put their clients' interests above their own.

*(Source: Dave Ramsey - A Better Retirement Plan for Our Hardworking Teachers)*

**Don't Miss Out on Educator Tax Deductions**
*The Balance* shares a helpful article about the Educator Expenses Tax Deduction. They explain that most things you spend money on as a teacher qualify for the deduction provided that you bought them for use in your classroom and your school or teacher's union has not reimbursed you for them. They must be "ordinary and necessary." This means they're items commonly accepted and used in a classroom and your students benefit from them.

Some common deductible expenses include:
>> Books
>> Supplies
>> Computer equipment, software, and services
>> Supplementary materials used in the classroom
>> Athletic equipment if it's used by health or physical education teachers
>> Professional development courses (2016 & later)

*to support your budgeting & investing goals*

**YOU NEED A BUDGET (YNAB):** This app takes a unique approach and helps you build your budget based on your income, and gives every dollar a job in your budget, like living expenses, savings and investments, etc. It forces you to think about every single dollar you spend.

**BUDGT:** This easy-to-use app creates a new budget for you based on how you've already spent each month.

**POCKETGUARD:** This app also links to all of your financial accounts, and tracks your spending and saving.

**EVERYDOLLAR:** Based on Dave's Baby Steps, this simple app tracks and helps you manage your finances with helpful visuals.

**MINT:** This popular app allows you to track your finances from your banks and helps you budget by categorizing transactions.

**MVELOPES:** This app follows the idea of putting cash into envelopes to plan your spending each month, except in a digital format.

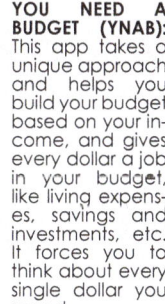

## time vs. money
## when to DIY & when to HIRE OUT

### Groceries
It's no surprise that our time, as teachers, is terribly limited, as well as one of our most treasured commodities. With this in mind, consider taking grocery shopping off your to-do list by paying a small fee for curbside pickup or delivery straight to your door. With Giant Eagle's Curbside Express, grocery delivery is only $5.95. Imagine what you could do with all of this free time and energy each week!

### Cooking
Many people now swear by meal prepping for each week. Whether you're feeding a family of 5, have specific dietary restrictions, or are on a tight budget, there are tons of food bloggers that share expert advice and recipes! Just head to Pinterest and search for your specific needs. If planning meals isn't for you, you can see if your budget allows you to take a simpler route. Try a meal delivery service. Popular options are HelloFresh, Blue Apron, Terra's Kitchen, and Sun Basket.

### Home Improvement
When you're a homeowner, it can seem like home improvement is a never ending job, as well as a never-ending expense. Lessen the financial burden by evaluating these three key considerations for each home project (advice from Scott McGillivray):
**Ability** – Be honest with yourself about what you can and cannot handle, without being overconfident about your skills.
**Cost** – Keep in mind that contractors often purchase materials at lower costs than individual homeowners, and if you make any mistakes you'll have to pay to fix them.
**Time** – What is your time worth, and how quickly do you want this project done?

### Clothing Shopping
Some people are born with a natural ability to put outfits together in both a stylish and flattering way. If you are not one of those people, make the decision to refrain from wasting time and money shopping for clothes that end up just being pushed to the back of your closet, and think about a service like Trunk Club or Stitch Fix. They pair you with a personal stylist and send curated looks straight to your door! Some are more affordable than most people think!

### Cleaning
Whether you love or hate doing the work, one thing we can all agree on is that we like a fresh, clean home. Take a moment to think about what chores you don't mind and what chores you absolutely dread. Can you delegate to someone else in your family? If not, request gift cards for a house cleaning next year. Amazon provides home cleaning services for things like deep cleaning, window cleaning, carpet cleaning, and more!

Teachers everywhere are constantly faced with the difficult decision to choose to DIY or hire out. So, how do you make that decision? Obviously, everyone is different, and has various skills and interests, but here are some ideas to consider.

### Your Own Mutual Fund

It can be a smart move to set up your own mutual fund on the side. These funds are a wise second option, since they are a collection of investments in both stocks and bonds. The blend of well-rounded investments can offer some security for your finances. You can generally customize your mutual fund to be more or less risky, based on your needs.

### How can you be sure you'll have enough?

People are living longer than ever. What was once a sufficient amount of money to retire will no longer get you through the expected years of your life.

Compared to just one century ago, our lives are an average of three decades longer now, particularly for women. In 1919, the female life expectancy was 56.0. Now, women can live well beyond 80 years, and this is likely to increase even more before most of the current workforce retires.

A guideline that experts offer is to assume that for each million dollars saved in your retirement account, you can expect between $40,000 and $50,000 as your yearly "salary" upon retiring. So if you want to maintain an income of $60,000, you will need your total amount in all retirement and investment accounts to net more than $1,000,000.

### What can you do to get there?

Here are some simple steps you can take today to get you closer to your retirement goals.

>> Set up an automatic transfer.
You can have pre-scheduled transactions go directly from your checking account into savings, a mutual fund, and other accounts automatically each month. Make this the first bill you pay, to yourself!

>> Check your recurring expenses.
Go through your bank statement, and highlight subscriptions that you do not use. It's easy to sign up and forget. Cancel the memberships, streaming programs, and accounts that you no longer use regularly. Write a note in your calendar to repeat this in six months.

>> Max out your "match."
Be sure that you put **at least** the amount that is matched for your retirement account. Over time, as you can increase this amount, continue to adjust it. Make this a yearly check, as you do your taxes.

*(Additional Sources: NEA, Berkeley.edu, EPI)*

# PODCASTS

### 1 teach and retire rich

Teacher Dan Otter, Ph.D. and Certified Financial Planner Scott Dauenhauer discuss retirement plans and give savings advice specifically for teachers! Their goal is to help educators navigate the complicated 403(b) and 457(b) plans, as well as pensions.

### 2 next gen personal finance

This podcast engages and empowers listeners to make ideal and informed financial decisions.

### 3 journey to launch

The host, Jamila, a Certified Financial Education Instructor helps listeners on their journey to achieve financial independence through becoming debt-free and budget-savvy.

### 4 you need a budget

This inspirational podcast shares personal stories of other YNAB followers who reached financial freedom.

**Brenna Quinlan**
>> teacher
>> illustrator
>> permaculture expert

Text, Illustrations, & Photos
by Brenna Quinlan

# L T U R E  *through art*

## creative passion

It seems to me that some people in this world have a burning desire to create. Maybe we're all born with it, and maybe some of us suppress it when, as children, we're told we can't sing or draw or write. But some make it through with an intense and obsessive passion for linking disparate ideas, representing information in novel ways, and exploring emotions and themes through their chosen medium. I draw, write and teach because there is no other way. From the time I wake up each morning until my dreams at night, I am scheming, thinking, planning, creating, and obsessively sketching, scrawling and note taking. Each idea that I deny weighs heavily on me. There have been times of my life when I haven't drawn much, and these were ghost-like days for me, where I felt I was denying part of who I was. Now that I draw and teach permaculture for a living, I am constantly in the creative headspace. It can be exhausting, but I'm committed to the adventure.

I don't think I've ever told anyone about my illustration process, so here goes. When I'm collaborating with or working for someone, they'll pitch an idea to me. These are as varied as the people I work for: some have it all figured out, with photos and sketches of every drawing they want in their compost book. Others have a vague idea that they'd like something about the mushroom cycle, but they're not really sure of what information they would like to be included. I take whatever ideas and direction they give me, and I draw up some sketches. This is the most creative part, as I find myself problem solving, trying out different combinations, deciding which kinds of native bees to include or which way the worm farm should be facing. Then I send those drafts in to the client. They get back to me with any changes they'd like, and I do a second draft. Once that gets the all clear, I draw up the images in pen. I then photocopy each image onto thicker paper that will take watercolour, and paint the drawings up. After that, I'll erase any splotches in photoshop, enhance the contrast, and send them off as high res jpegs to their new owners. The originals end up on my wall in a rotating exhibition that I have going, so I can see all of the work I've done recently. And then, weeks or months down the track, I'll see the finished book, or the printed poster, and the illustration job will be complete.

I had always considered myself an artist, and my focus during uni was on portraiture and realism. I moved here to Melliodora Permaculture Gardens in Central Victoria in early 2017, and spent a few months as an intern, learning about gardening, low waste living, goats and chooks, and all other aspects of the permie lifestyle. I'd draw in secret, assuming that no one else was interested in seeing my art. The whole time I was interning, my then volunteer host David Holmgren (co-originator of the permaculture concept) was talking about a ground-breaking new book that he'd been working on for years. It was only a few months away from being published. I'd strain my ears each time someone mentioned a tiny detail of this book, and from the little I'd heard, it was set to be an amazing work. Then one day in June, their illustrator pulled out of the project for personal reasons. He had seen some of my drawings online, and he'd recommended me. From one day to the next, I became David Holmgren's illustrator. To be honest, I'd spent so much time living in rural South America where luxury career titles (illustrators, graphic designers, textile artists) are pretty tough to come by, that I wasn't even sure I knew what an illustrator was. But I came up to speed pretty quickly; I had a deadline of three months to complete 130 complex technical drawings, each requiring between five and ten revisions as the text and flow of the book changed to match my input. It was a huge few months. I didn't know the first thing about photoshop, I didn't own a printer or scanner…I didn't even own pens. Since Retrosuburbia was launched in February 2018, I've had a steady avalanche of permaculture-themed work raining down on me. I feel very fortunate that I was in the right place at the right time to kick off my illustration career in such a way.

Brenna Quinlan, an illustrator and teacher in Australia, uses watercolor to educate the world about permaculture. She has travelled extensively and now teaches and coordinates permaculture courses. Learn more by following her instagram account where she shares her passion for permaculture education through art.

@brenna_quinlan

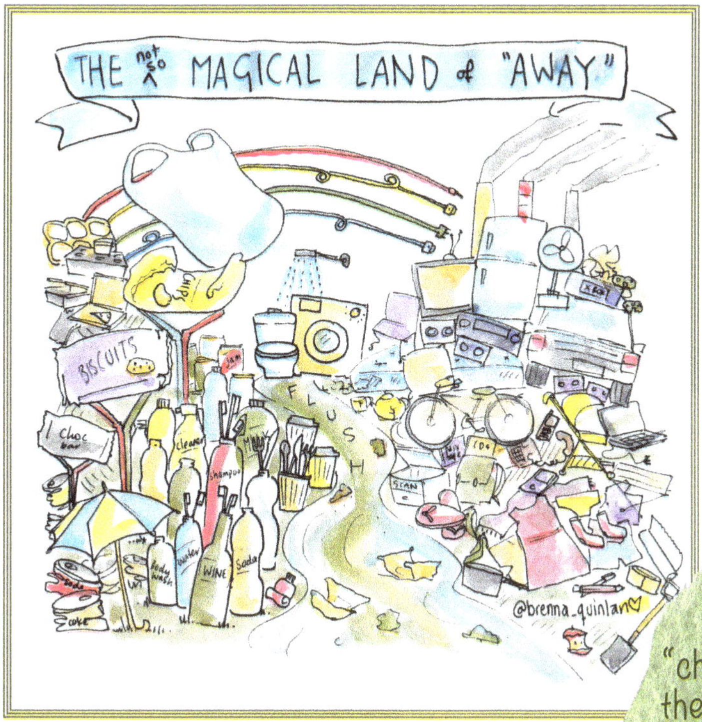


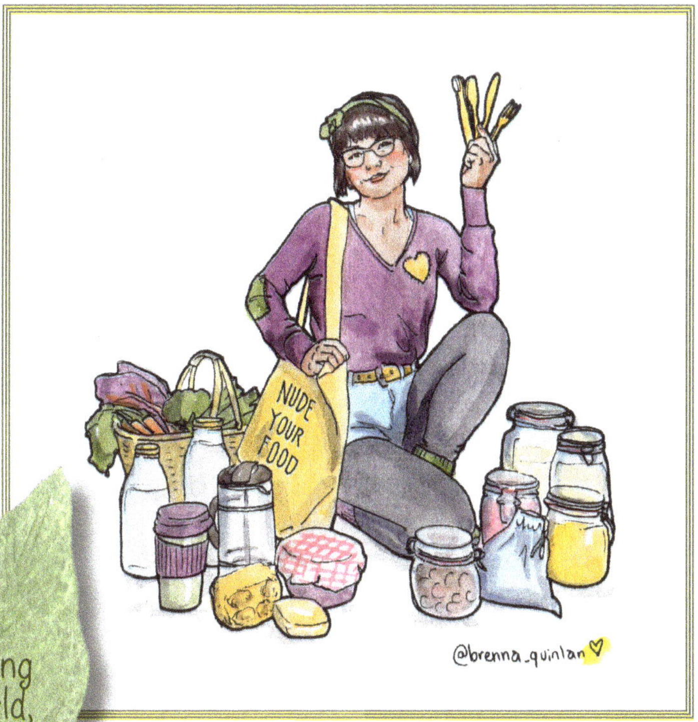


"changing the world, one drawing at a time"

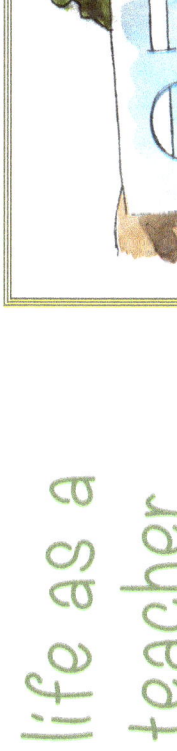

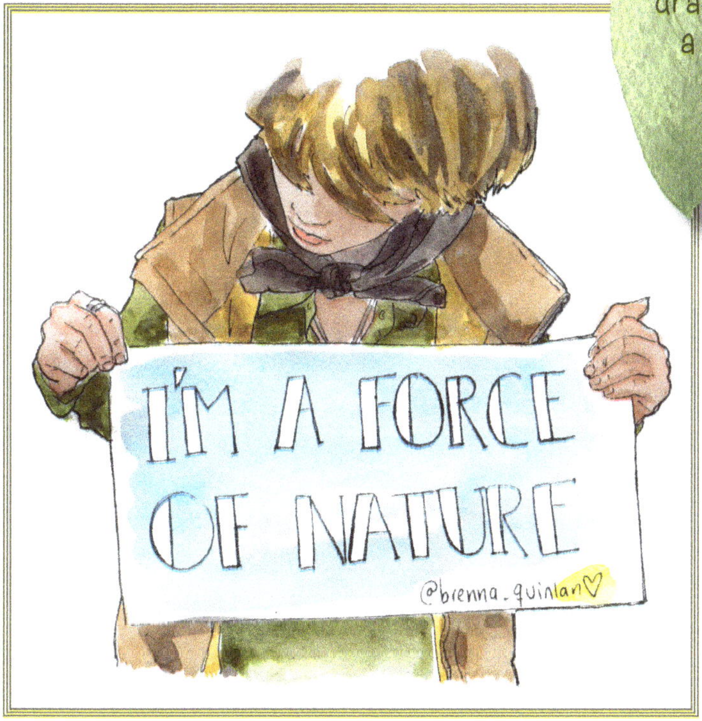


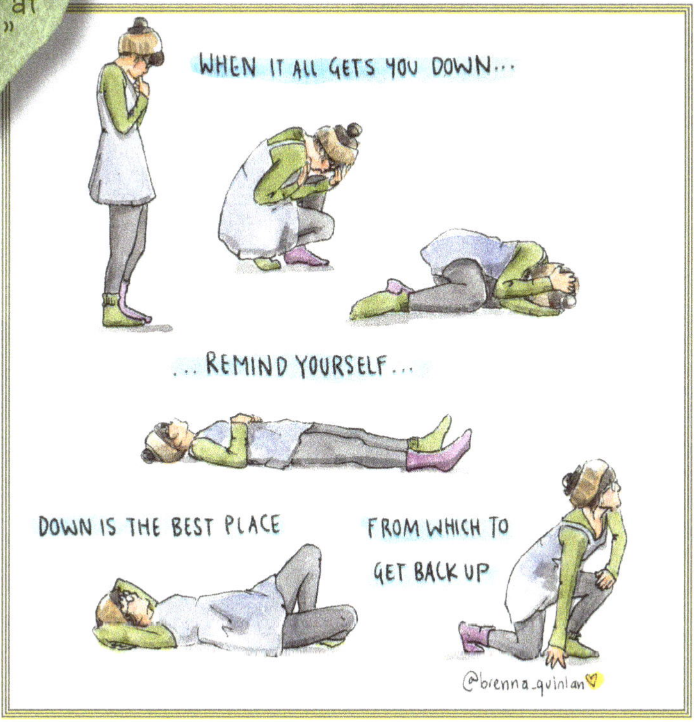


## life as a teacher

I'm far from mastering the work/life balance, but I've been putting a lot of energy into figuring it out. As a freelance illustrator and educator, sometimes I feel like I'm running two full-time jobs. Dan Palmer's work on Holistic Decision Making has helped me to identify my northern arrow, my moral compass, as it were. Now each time I decide if I'll take on a job or go and do something for someone, I check if it's taking me in the direction I want to go in. The problem is...there are so many meaningful and exciting projects out there. I'm still practicing saying no. Creatives, teachers, parents and community members hold such power to influence those around them in this context of climate change and biodiversity loss. There is a growing movement for those with a voice to use it wisely in the face of our changing world, and I find it incredibly encouraging to see teachers stepping up, researching and educating themselves, and passing that information on to their students. It's the children who will reach adulthood in a very different world from the one we enjoy today, and assisting their resilience and competence to face these challenges is a task that teachers all over the world are increasingly putting their minds to.

"I need to see trees and sky from my desk, and stars from my bed. I need to have wild spaces to walk through, explore, and forage in, to centre me... I need to be able to wander around and eat fat plums straight off the tree and forage weeds for a salad lunch. The property where I live feeds my body, my soul and my mind, and I wouldn't have it any other way."

*travel, experience, nature, and community*

There are a few things I've done in life that I didn't think I'd be capable of doing. After uni, I took off with a one way ticket to India, and decided I'd stay away until I found what i was looking for. I was gone for six years. Being a long-term traveller, I learned to live without money. I went for three of those years without paying a cent for accommodation. I foraged and traded most of my food, and made friends wherever I went so that I never felt alone. I hitch hiked for four months across the United States. Then I got on a second-hand bicycle and rode 11,000 kilometres from Kelowna in Canada all the way to the Panama Canal. It took me 11 months. I learned Spanish along the way, and eventually fell in with a group of 'permies' (i.e. people who do and live permaculture) in Argentina, where I began teaching permaculture and natural construction. I lived with them in community for over a year. I came back to Australia at the end of 2016 to see my family, and have been here ever since. That trip seems so far away now.

the Tea House

I live at Melliodora, the one hectare permaculture demonstration site created by co-originator of the permaculture concept David Holmgren and his partner Su Dennett. There are three houses on the property: the big house where Dave and Su live, the medium house that the folks from Milkwood permaculture call home, and the tiny house, known as the Tea House, where I live. I draw at my desk, looking through the floor-to-ceiling windows out over the dam and the quince trees towards the escarpment. This space fills me with happiness and inspiration.

I need to see trees and sky from my desk, and stars from my bed. I need to have wild spaces to walk through, explore, and forage in, to centre me when I feel stressed. I need the routine of milking the goats in frosty winter mornings and diving into the dam on hot summer afternoons. I need to be able to wander around and eat fat plums straight off the tree and forage weeds for a salad lunch. The property where I live feeds my body, my soul and my mind, and I wouldn't have it any other way.

We tend to get sucked into the way that we 'should' be living: paying down the mortgage, buying a fancy car, going on expensive holidays that we need because we work so hard. But a growing trend in living simply is liberating people from all of this noise, and helping them to rediscover what they would really rather be spending their lives doing. If you're feeling that you don't have enough time to create, maybe it's time to reassess some of the things we take for granted in life. For me, if money is standing in the way of creativity, then I need to spend less so I can earn less and spend my time doing what makes me happy (and what makes the world a better place) instead.

Brenna teaching a Permaculture Course

To explore Brenna's work with permaculture education through illustration, visit brennaquinlan.com

## pegboard shelves

We followed a DIY from Vintage Revivals, and cut them to the dimensions that we needed. These moved with me from my last classroom, so they are super sturdy & functional. I change out the decor on them to coordinate with whatever we're learning at the time. This seating area is a student favorite, and the cabinet "doors" I had my husband add are a great way to hide all the junk!

## Megan Rowe's Classroom
calm • flexible • structured

text and photography by Megan Rowe

**functioning systems**

**inviting vibes**

**organized flexibility**

When my classroom and my home are in an orderly fashion, I'm able to be more focused and complete the tasks that I'm working on. In order to keep things organized, I live by the motto that "everything has a home!"

### @ ohmeganrowe
### 4th grade

Social Studies
Science
Math

## appealing design

I have a passion for design and creating an inviting space was my main goal for my classroom. As a teacher, I work best in a place that's organized, appealing and flexible, so I wanted to create a space that's just that for my students. I love design and all that comes with it. I'm a tad bit OCD, so finding ways to make functioning systems that are also appealing to the eye just gives me all the feels.

At the front of my classroom, I have a computer teacher area that's connected to my SMART board. I utilize this space for my whole group lessons. In the back corner of my classroom, I have a horseshoe table where I meet with my small groups. This area serves as my "desk".

## prioritizing family

As a teacher, it's easy to get consumed with all of the to dos. My husband, Chad, and I have two boys, Hudson (6) and Thomas (3) who are the lights of our life. Spending time with our family is our favorite thing to do! Family is my number one priority, and one of the reasons I became a teacher. I love that my work schedule meshes so well with my children's schedules. Hudson will be starting Kindergarten this year on my campus, and I just can't wait to have him with me at work everyday. In order to keep a good balance, I utilize every minute I have at school being productive and implementing systems so that my daily to dos don't consume too much of my time.

 You can never have enough storage in a classroom! This shelf and desk area serves as storage for more flexible seating options (lap desks, clipboards, bar stools, etc.) while also functioning as the computer station in the classroom.

These bar height tables are a hit in my classroom. The students love to work at these, and I've actually included them as an incentive in my positive behavior plan.

## 5 Slick Teacher Hacks

*from megan*

1. Download the Honey Google Extension - it automatically looks for coupons from whatever store you're shopping at online.

2. Make an "end of day routine" for yourself to help you prep for the upcoming day. Mine is to get bell work ready, change my station slides, sharpen pencils, rotate my station chart, (this tells the student what station they are going to and changes daily) and put out tomorrow's supplies/assignments.

3. Knot up your t-shirts to add a little "spunk" to your jeans & t-shirt days. Adding a vest or cardigan helps too!

4. Date your spouse. My husband and I have a scheduled date night every other week during the school year.

5. Bringing in faux plants to your classroom is a great way to make it more inviting.

Flexible seating classrooms are the best. I'm always trying to implement "choice" into my classroom environment, so flexible seating was a no brainer. Students are able to try out all of the types of seating to see which they feel is the most comfortable for them.

*the color scheme*

## teacher corner o>>>>

Here's our classroom calendar (a modern take) and my computer/teacher area. This custom built desk is not only a space saver; it's also appealing to the eye, which is a must for me.

## finding the items

I am an avid online shopper, and Amazon is one of my favorite places to grab things. I'm a prime member, so the quick shipping is awesome! Target, Wal-Mart & Ikea are some of my other favorite teacher spots.

## quick tip

Something I tried this year and loved was zip-tying my groups of desks together. It kept the floor plan of my classroom in tact, not allowing the desks to slide around. Genius!

## creative hack o>>>>

I love to bring outside pieces into my classroom, but I also love to utilize what I'm given. Removing the legs from the desks is a great way to offer a different type of seating without spending any money!

See more on Megan's instagram at @ohmeganrowe

### gratitude

#### What are you most grateful for?

I have the most supportive administrative staff and colleagues that strive to make our school an amazing place for our students. There's something so special about Forest Ridge Elementary and I'm lucky to get to call it my school home!

### students

#### What do your students love most in here?

My students' favorite thing about our classroom is the flexible seating that's available to them. They enjoy trying out the different areas and being able to make the space their own.

### self

#### What do you love most about this room?

I love the organization and inviting feel that my room provides for all of our visitors. It's truly one of my favorite places to spend time.

# Boost Productivity & Work Less
## *by strategically coordinating with your cycle*

**How to get better results with less time and effort by embracing your body's natural cycles**

**Male vs. Female Hormone Cycles and the Impact They Have on Productivity**

Productivity concepts tend to revolve around a workday. There is a natural "morning" energy phase, a noon-time "transition" that shifts us into the second half of the day, and then an afternoon "decline" that eases into the end of the work day. The evening is then for rest, to reflect, recover, and prepare for the next day.

This design works well for male brains, which naturally follow a consistent pattern. Mens' hormones peak in the morning, and then slowly drop off leading into each evening. However, female hormone patterns extend over a 28 day cycle. The hormonal flow that spreads over an entire month for women is compacted into an equivalent (but different) hormone flow for men that repeats every single day.

This means that we need to re-think the female work flow. Give yourself permission to work within the seasons of your natural energy shifts. By embracing the way that hormones impact the brain, you can be happier and more efficient at the same time.

Just as many males can do deep, focused work all morning long, but then have a dip in productivity throughout the afternoon, females can push through at top performance for a solid week, then have a dip during the end phase of their biological cycles.

Both patterns result in amazing output, but in different cycle lengths. The male brain goes through its hormone shift every 24 hours, while the female brain takes 28 days. Here's how to stop working against this pattern. Work in tune with your body to plan your tasks and to-do lists strategically throughout a month. The payoff? Less time overall spent working, with the same result. And you'll save yourself the frustration of trying to tackle jobs that are not suited for your current brain chemistry as a bonus.

### The Four Natural Phases

Female bodies simply do not operate in a pattern that makes every day the same. Ignoring the natural rhythm can only bring challenges as the mind and body resist each other. Being aware of the phases, and knowing that they affect both the body and the brain, will allow you to harness the power of the peaks in the cycle and embrace the valleys.

You already know how the pre-menstrual phase affects your brain, mood, and body. But the other phases are also characterized by different hormonal shifts that impact your brain as well.

During the follicular phase (beginning on day 1 of your cycle), the balance of brain chemicals leads you slowly from a reflective mindset into a creative one. As estrogen levels slowly rise, you are open to new ideas and are able to come up with solutions, designs, and ideas that may not come so easily at other times.

As your body approaches the ovulation phase, you become more approachable to others, biologically speaking. Your verbal skills are stronger than they are in any other phase. It's the ideal time for emotional thinking, empathy, and a mothering instinct.

The luteal phase is a longer portion of the cycle, in which the drop in estrogen and rise of progesterone cause your brain to be wired for getting things done. You are clear-headed and can focus and persevere through challenging tasks.

Knowing these patterns can help you direct your efforts more efficiently. Don't fight it! You will not be at your peak for every type of task on any given day. When you have a long term set of to-dos, try using the guide on the next page to select, schedule, and plan ahead.

Teachers need to save every hour of effort and frustration that they can. By choosing the right time for each task, you will cut down on the overall time spent and avoid spinning your wheels.

> Hormones get no respect. We think of them as the elusive chemicals that make us a bit moody, but these magical little molecules do so much more. >> Susannah Cahalan

*Work **with** your body's natural hormone cycles of rest phases and focused work phases instead of **against** them.*

# How to Harness the Power of You

Take time for a craft or hobby.

Design the labels for all those cute classroom storage bins.

Dream up a creative solution for that class that just can't get their homework completion rate up.

Work on your bulletin boards.

Set up a time to get together with the principal for the conversation or question you've been putting off dealing with. Schedule it for next week, when you are in the communication zone.

Write your classroom newsletter.

Throw that class party.

Set up your fundraising page while your words will come across clearly and you are more likely to inspire "yes" answers.

Call a parent you've been needing to have a nice long chat with.

*estrogen*

Day 1 of Period

## follicular phase
### *creativity*

Hormones are low, and it's a great time to try new things and think outside the box. As estrogen slowly rises, this is the best time to address your creative tasks. Get that big painting project done now, and design those cards for the Sunshine Committee. Tasks like this would take you twice as long and bring you extra frustration later! During this phase, you'll be more inspired for the crafty tasks and enjoy these jobs more.

## ovulation phase
### *communication*

The increase in estrogen is accompanied by energy and positivity. The blend of hormones here leads your brain toward excellent communication skills. Verbal skills are strongest here, and your ideas come across as more appealing. Now is the time to tackle a tricky parent-teacher conference you've been dreading, or have a one-on-one with the student who really needs your personal attention. Reach out to a co-teacher for collaboration during this time too.

*Flowers do not bloom in all four seasons. Your body is not designed to either.*

# Hormonal Cycles for Productivity

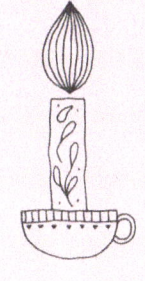

- Organize that classroom library.
- Grade those essay tests.
- Work on your curriculum map.
- Put your head down and get that seating chart done, no matter what it takes.
- Plow through the rest of that google classroom coursework you still need to finish up.
- Go through the whole checklist to review which standards you still need to cover.
- Gather all the links to finish up your first escape room activity.
- Make a batch of rubrics...
- ...Make a batch of cookies!
- Put on your favorite show or podcast and just let your mind relax while you sharpen sixteen sets of colored pencils.
- Reflect, then set goals for next month.
- Grab a glass of wine and some candles. Browse pinterest in search of awesome classroom inspiration.

*progesterone*

*testosterone*

## luteal phase
*focus*

The luteal phase is a very powerful time, when productivity peaks. Progesterone is increasing, allowing you to feel driven and have a clear mind. The brain chemistry here is ideal for detail-oriented tasks. Handle your more grueling tasks here, that you put off during your creative phase. You will not want to deal with them next week as you head into pre-menstruation. Any administrative to-dos, mountains of paperwork, or big projects are your best bet during this phase. Get down to the nitty gritty and execute on all those big ideas you dreamed up earlier this month!

## pre-menstruation phase
*reflection*

Your motivation may start to dwindle as you head into the next menstrual phase. Hormones drop back off and lead into a "winter" of your cycle. You'll crave down time. Don't plan any big meetings or long nights of grading papers during this week. Your body may force you to take a bit of a break. Luckily, your brain is now ready for reflection, introspection, and intuition right now. Use your restful evenings to review how your classes have been doing, ponder your performance, and reflect on what is going well and what may need a fresh approach soon. This may just lead into a brainstorm next follicular phase!

*loving snowday? Snap a pic and share on social*

# peppermint essential oil | HACKS & USES

The peppermint plant, which came from a blend of spearmint and water mint, has been cultivated for a wide variety of medicinal benefits for thousands of years. It has been proven to have antimicrobial effects that help us fight oral pathogens. It's uses in oral heath are widely known. But more uses for peppermint have been found over the years. It offers relief for ailments including muscle discomfort, joint pain, headaches, nausea, and allergies. It even offers skin protection.

Essential oils are made by extracting certain ingredients from the flowering plant. These oils contain VOCs, meaning that they give off chemical emmisions and must be treated with care. Do not diffuse peppermint oil without learning how to do it carefully, and use caution even when applying it to skin. Do plenty of research before starting if you plan to use it around children or pets. Although it is one of the most popular oils, it contains menthol and phenol, and can be dangerous if not used properly.

Peppermint is best used topically with a carrier oil. If you plan to apply it to the skin, blend it with almond or jojoba oil for best results. It can cause a burning sensation if you put the drops straight into a bath or directly onto your skin.

To freshen breath, place a drop of peppermint oil under your toungue, then drink a glass of water.

Ease nausea or motion sickness by either smelling the oil, or rubbing it (with carrier oil) on wrists or abdomen. Battle sinus troubles or allergies by rubbing it on the chest or temples.

**A SINGLE DROP OF PEPPERMINT ESSENTIAL OIL IS EQUIVALENT TO MORE THAN 25 CUPS OF PEPPERMINT TEA.**

Apply a roller containing peppermint oil blended with a carrier oil on the forehead, temples, or back of the neck for instant migraine relief. Be careful to avoid the eyes.

Refresh yourself when you feel tired or stressed by adding a diluted blend of peppermint oil to a bath. Try adding lavender oil for an even more relaxing experience.

Keep ants, mosquitoes, and bees outside the edge borders of your outdoor living spaces by spraying a blend of vinegar and peppermint oil on deck umbrellas, outdoor rugs, and entrances.

Add peppermint oil to your shampoo. It has anti-inflammatory properties and will absorb extra oils on the scalp. The peppermint essential oil acts as an antiseptic, helps moisturize hair, promotes growth, and even fights dandruff.

Put a few drops at the bottom of your trash bin, in your unscented bottle of all-purpose cleaner, or in your massage oil for an energizing and pleasant scent.

@docoopteaching

# DISCOVER

Everything you had no idea you were missing!

@molecularmotifs

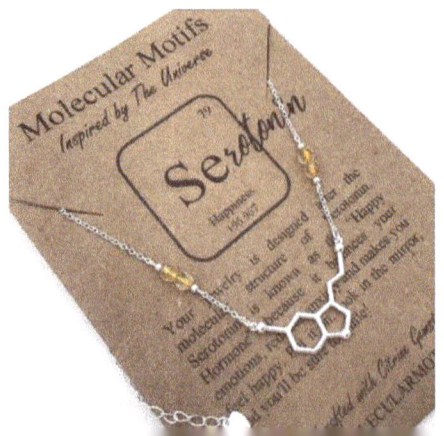

@littlerayofsunflower

1 >> Dr. Jenna Copper, an educational expert, teaches high school and college. She provides insights for ELA teachers as well as ed. tech resources and hacks that work for a wide range of courses and grade levels. Follow her on instagram @doccopteaching for creative strategies and a beautiful balance of teacher and family life.

2 >> Lacy is a mom, artist, and blogger who shares home decor ideas, recipes, and plenty of crafty DIYs. Get inspired by her peaceful home on instagram @livingawilderlife where she shares real life stories, solutions, and style.

3 >> We've found what is sure to become your new favorite gift idea for any colleague, and maybe even some relatives! The jewelry designs from @molecularmotifs are such a unique choice. There are gorgeous options for any teacher's interests, including DNA designs, golden ratios for math teachers, catnip molecules for cat lovers, new "STEMinist" bracelets, music notes, and even caffeine, bourbon and chocolate molecules formed into necklaces.

4 >> Raya, a paper artist from Barcelona, makes delicate and intricate paper crafts. Follow @littlerayofsunflower on instagram for creative inspiration and close-up peeks at the work of a papercrafting master. (Art by Raya Sader Bujana, Photos by Leo Garcia Mendez)

# 5 PODCAST PICKS FOR TEACHERS

Jennifer from the **Cult of Pedagogy** podcast is an intelligent and engaging host with thoughtful insights on education topics like dress code, higher order thinking, equity, leveled texts, and more.

**Making Math Moments that Matter,** a podcast by Kyle Pearce and Jon Orr, offers conversations that act as coaching calls for educators struggling with challenges specific to teaching math. (Grades K-12)

Your students will be thrilled to have classroom podcast time with **Brains On**, a science podcast that will make them giggle, learn, and even guess mystery sounds as they explore fun topics.

The Google Educator Trainers behind the **Teaching, Brewed** podcast chat about tech and other issues relevant to teachers with a goal of encouraging conversation, reflection, and innovation. (for specialists & general ed.)

**But Why** podcast takes real questions from kids, even tackling the tough stuff, like "What's it like to be an adult," and "Why do people get cancer?" with thoughtful responses geared toward young minds.

# CONSCIOUS LIVING
## A husband & wife teacher team sound off on balancing it all

**GETTING CRAFTY**
I made the earring holders by hot gluing cross stitch backing to picture frames and Phil added the hooks to a shelf to hold all of my necklaces.

Phil and April manage a beautiful balancing act. Both are teachers, but Phil also manages the joys and pressures of coaching Texas football. April prioritizes a healthy lifestyle for her family, and still finds time to teach toxin-free living to other women online. They do it all without sacrificing health or keeping up a beautiful home and happy children.

How do they tackle the challenges of daily life, both at home, and at school?

They're sharing insights on balancing teaching, family, home decor, organization, healthy eating, hobbies, and more. It's the little things that all add up to keep running a happy, healthy family among the challenges of a teacher lifestyle.

I like to say that my hobbies are at least productive, because if all goes well, everyone gets to eat well or we end up with a new piece of furniture.

## DAILY ROUTINES

**So as a two-teacher family, what makes it all work for you? Tell us about your strategies for managing mornings. How has it shifted over time, and through the phases of life?**

APRIL: When the kids were younger, I tried to get up a bit earlier so I was ready before they woke up. When this worked out perfectly, it helped to make the mornings easier, but let's face it, there were more times the kids were up before I was ready for them to be. When this happened, I often just had the kids sit with me in the bathroom while I finished getting ready. They would play with a few toys or look at books. Connor often liked to get in the tub and pretend to drive it. Now that they are older and more self-sufficient, we have them help make their lunches and lay out their clothes the night before. They are both also old enough now to make their own breakfast, so this helps a ton with busy mornings! To this day, we are still usually rushing out the door, but that's probably my fault for hitting the snooze button too many times!

**What are your best tips for managing homework time when EVERYONE in the family has homework??**

PHIL: When everyone has homework, we divide and conquer. We will try to help the kids take care of theirs first. Usually I will help with the Math/Science stuff if needed, and April will help with the Reading and Writing as well as signing and filling out the numerous administrative forms that come home. We encourage the kids to use their time wisely and to get homework started in April's classroom after school, while they wait for her to be finished working. If they don't get done, they finish it while dinner is cooking, with us jumping back and forth between the table where they are working and the stove where dinner is cooking.

Once we have finished dinner, we try to get the kitchen cleaned up quickly so that April and I can start on any work that needs to be done around the house or prepping material for the next work day. During this time the kids quietly occupy themselves (in theory) and then start to get ready for bed.

## APRIL

teacher

health conscious mom

toxin free living expert

## PHIL

coach

dad

barbecuer of meats

**Do you have any bedtime stratgies to recommend?**

PHIL: I often find letting them know that they have 10-15 minutes left before bed helps there to be less whining.

We also put them to bed soon enough to leave time to chat. This helps because they know they don't technically have to go to sleep right away and it's something we all look forward to as its the last few minutes we get to spend with each other for the day so we try to make it special. This may be us asking them what their favorite thing from the day was or sometimes April will leave them with some affirmations before they drift off to sleep like, "You are smart, You are kind, You are hardworking," etc.

Sometimes she will say things like "I love you like syrup loves pancakes" or "I love you like bears love honey" It's silly, but the kids love it and hopefully it will be a good memory for them.

Then they each pick a song for us to sing. It's usually Jesus Loves me for Connor and Twinkle, Twinkle Little Star for Kailee. It's been the same two songs for the last several years! Lastly we say prayers and kiss goodnight.

**You've both shifted gears as teachers. How did the career transitions impact you both?**

APRIL: I taught second grade at the same school for 6 years, but when we moved recently to a new school district, I obtained a position in kindergarten. I wasn't sure what to expect, but knew I wanted to try teaching a different grade level, so I went into it with an open mind. For me and my family, this change was a blessing for many reasons. To start, the school staff was so welcoming. I felt comfortable being myself from the very first interview, which was a surprise because that process is normally a very nerve wracking thing for me! My new kinder team was also a great fit. We all get along really well, help each other out and spend a good amount of time laughing with one another.

More importantly, I found the joy of teaching again! My years in second grade were starting to weigh me down. There was so much stress and pressure from the constant grades, not only on me, but my students too. The anxiety and tears I often saw in my students broke my heart. I didn't feel this was how it is supposed to be in these early primary grades, but with kinder all of that disappeared. With tons of tests out of the way, the stress and anxiety went away and we had time to just focus on making the learning fun and engaging like it is supposed to be.

I also found out that I absolutely love this age group. Their curiosity about everything, and the excitement and love they brought to my classroom made me smile every single day. This translated into a happier me at home: something I am sure my family is extremely grateful for. I tell my husband all the time, I am so happy and never want to teach another grade ever again!

## CAREER TRANSITIONS

PHIL: Over the 11 years that I have been teaching and coaching in Texas, my career has evolved from teaching all math classes to more of a coaching focus and teaching a few health classes. While there are days that I miss delivering a great math lesson, these changes have allowed me to devote more time and have greater impact with the people I am most passionate about; namely, the players I coach and my family. The time once spent offering PreCalculus tutorials before and after school is now devoted to making sure our student-athletes are being successful in their classes and attending the tutorials they should be. All the long hours spent grading math tests on Sunday nights after working all day preparing the gameplan for Friday night, are now reserved for Family Game Night or other quality time with April, Kailee and Connor.

## PLANNING HEALTHY MEALS

*Chocolate Chunk Banana Squares*

*Chocolate Over Night No Oats*

*Banana Blueberry Bread*

*Berry Chocolate Almond Butter Smoothie*

*Healthy chocolate chip donuts*

APRIL: I do most of the meal planning at our house, but on the weekend we sit down together and discuss our schedules for the upcoming week so we can figure out which days we will both be home or days that one of us will be working late. This helps us plan which days I will cook, which days we will have left-overs or which days Phil can help out with the cooking. From there, if I am in need of a new recipe, I'll start searching for ones that are quick, healthy, low carb, etc., whatever we may be needing for the week. I do save all of the recipes I've cooked in the past and that we have loved in the notes app on my phone, so sometimes all I need to do is check out my list and pick from there.

Once I have my recipes, I create my shopping list and during the school year I will order my groceries online and pick up on Sunday. This truly saves so much time for busy teachers and I find I spend way less money than when I go into the store (especially if my kids are with me). My goal is usually to aim for only cooking three meals a week that will provide leftovers for the days we are too busy or too tired to cook. Sometimes this means doubling a recipe in order to ensure we will have leftovers. This helps save us a lot of time during the busy work week because then we essentially have meals for 6 days, but only had to cook 3. The other day, Phil will usually cook or we may decide to go out to dinner. Another tip that helps our family eat healthy, home cooked meals all week is meal prepping. Now, I don't always have time on the weekend to do this, but when I do it is really helpful for the following week because it saves a lot of time on those busy school days and helps keep our healthy eating habits on track.

**April shares her recipes for her easy to-go breakfasts on instagram:**

**@consciouslivinginspired**

# APRIL'S 4 EASY TOXIN-FREE SWAPS

These are applied and absorbed by your body's largest organ, the skin. This is why I recommend making these swaps first when switching to a more toxin free lifestyle.

**>> Deodorant**
Scully's, Vermont Soap Company, and Bend Soap Company are all great options with minimal ingredients.

**>> Body Wash**
Our whole family loves to use a charcoal body bar! You can find out more about this bar and where to purchase it from in my facebook group *Conscious Living Inspired*.

**>> Lotion**
I am currently loving Billie Lotion, but Carina Organics is another favorite of mine!

**>> Fragrance**
Skylar fragrance is amazing and all the scents smell so good! You can get a sample pack of all 6 scents for $20 and then that can be applied to a full size bottle of your choice!

**Do you have any advice for the crazy hour after dinner? Who pitches in for cleanup?**

APRIL: After dinner is a team effort to help get things cleaned up quickly so we can all relax and spend the rest of our evening together. Phil is a master at washing the items that need to be hand washed since he grew up without a dishwasher. He can wash the dishes in no time, while I would be there twice as long, so we leave that task for him.

The kids help out by emptying or loading the dishwasher and since we try to have a toxin free home, we feel comfortable letting them sanitize the counters because we know they will not be exposed to any harmful toxins when using the safe products we have in our home. Now don't get me wrong, we are nowhere near perfect at this. There are days that we are just too exhausted from the long work day to clean up. So the dishes go in the sink and we get to it the next day or the day after that. For me, this is something that I had to learn not to let stress me out.

I've really had to change my mindset by reminding myself that when both parents work, the time is limited so everything isn't going to get done in one day and that's okay! We both try to remind ourselves on those super busy work days that there are more important things to tend to than the dishes. So some days that means leaving the kitchen a mess so we can have time with each other, have time to help the kids with their homework, have time that Phil can read Harry Potter to them, or have time to take them for a bike ride.

**That's so nice that you can have the kids clean and know they are not soaking up any harmful toxins. What led to your passion for "conscious" living?**

APRIL: After I had Connor, we began to exercise more and eat healthier by eating clean, whole foods that are naturally a part of this earth. This was also around the same time when buying organic began to become very popular so I decided to look into what made organic produce so different from conventional. I learned that non-organic produce is heavily covered in pesticides and a lot of it can't be washed off, so you're ingesting harmful chemicals that can cause health concerns over time. It seemed to me I wasn't doing my health or my family's health justice if we were trying to eat healthier, but consuming pesticides at the same time.

# CONSCIOUS CHOICES

This quickly became extremely important to me so from then on we switched to buying organic products as often as we could. After that, I started to pay more attention to the ingredient labels. I discovered that I couldn't even pronounce some of the ingredients and didn't even know what they were. I began to research these unknown ingredients and came to find out a lot of them were preservatives that were linked to endocrine disruption, developmental and reproductive toxicity and cancer.

The knowledge I gained and still continue to learn has led me to believe that a lot of the diseases that seem to be becoming more prevalent probably have a lot to do with pesticides, harmful additives in our foods, the chemicals in the everyday products we use in our home, and the unavoidable toxins in our environment. Over time, this all manifested into a more toxin-free lifestyle for our family. We now purchase organic produce, buy products with natural, minimal ingredients, cook and bake things from scratch, use toxin free bath/body products and household cleaners, and I even switched to toxin free makeup and skincare.

**Are you able to incorporate any toxin free choices into your classroom too?**

I like to use Dr. Bronner's hand sanitizer and Norwex cloths instead of Clorox wipes for the tables and my desk. These both help keep things clean and the germs away without all the harsh toxins found in traditional cleaning products.

> *I've really had to change my mindset by reminding myself that when both parents work, the time is limited so everything isn't going to get done in one day and that's okay!*

**How would you describe your home style? And how do you keep everyone organized?**

I'd say our style has a slight contemporary, rustic, farmhouse touch to it, but I am no design expert so I am not sure which exactly it falls under. I typically get my decorating ideas from pinterest and then try to recreate it on a two teacher income budget. This means a lot of shopping at Kohls, Target, and Hobby Lobby. Some of the rooms in our house are multi functional, like our bedroom. It's kind of a free for all in there, but serves many purposes. There is a space for me to ride my bike and to store all my workout equipment, a place for the dog to sleep when we aren't at home, a spot for me to do my makeup, a place to sleep, of course, and a couple of spaces for all my jewelry.

I made the earring holders by hot gluing cross stitch backing to picture frames and Phil added the hooks to a shelf to hold all of my necklaces. Upstairs in the loft is the kids area. We utilize shelves and totes to organize all of the toys and the lego tables from IKEA were a great bonus to help keep the area picked up. My two favorite places I recently decorated is the foyer and the collage wall in the dining room and we absolutely love the cozy feel to our living room.

Favorite Family Games:

Splendor

Tiki Topple

Dominos

Game night is pretty crazy for us. Our coaching staff stays with our players until we leave for the game, so 'dinner' for me is usually some type of sandwich that I eat around 3:30 or 4:00. We watch film, prepare for the game, share motivational words, and enjoy being together as a team.

April and the kids will usually pick up something quick on the way to the game, because April's energy usually goes to preparing something for the coaches to eat at our house after the game. Most weeks, we invite the coaches over to our house after we get back from the game. This is a time for us to celebrate if warranted or to share each other's disappointment if the game went the other way. Also, we are usually starving after the long game day. April comes through with some type of meal that she has prepared ahead of time and has ready for us when we arrive after getting all the players out of the fieldhouse and taking care of our other responsibilities. The coaches greatly appreciate April's efforts to feed us late in the night, and her tacos earn rave reviews. A few coaches even refused to believe that they hadn't been catered from a restaurant. Gameday is always hectic and I am blessed to be able to rely on April to take care of feeding everyone so that I can focus my attention on winning the game.

# GAME DAYS

### Phil's Pandora Stations:

>> Turnpike Troubadours Radio

>> Texas Country Radio

>> Pop & Hip Hop Power Workout

>> Summer Hits of the 90's Radio

# HOBBIES THAT DO DOUBLE DUTY

**What do you each enjoy during those rare moments of down time? Tell us any hobbies or self-care you make sure to fit in.**

APRIL: I love to bake healthy breakfast items or desserts that have clean, minimal ingredients. It brings my heart so much joy to know that there is nothing processed, no artificial food dyes, no harmful preservatives, in the treats we enjoy. The best part is they taste delicious, are full of ingredients with so many health benefits and the kids love them too!

PHIL: Two things I really enjoy doing outside of work are barbecuing and building furniture from wood. I have always enjoyed cooking, but my love of barbecuing really took off a few years ago when I got my first wood smoker. Now, whenever I have the time, I can be found in the backyard smoking a beef brisket or a few racks of ribs.

I have also made a few wooden tables for our house. April and I designed an entertainment stand that fit what we wanted and we worked together to create it. I like to say that my hobbies are at least productive, because if all goes well, everyone gets to eat well or we end up with a new piece of furniture.

both home made!

**Can you leave us with a favorite book recommendation?**

APRIL: *Choose Joy*, and *Joy for all Seasons- a weekly devotion*. These help me to have a positive outlook for the week.

*For more conscious living tips and toxin-free swaps, follow along on facebook in April's "Conscious Living Inspired" group.*

### DON'T MISS THE NEXT ISSUE

**Get notifications from Snowday Magazine by registering for our emails at snowdaymagazine.com**

### BONUS

We will send you our free minimag too!

### P.S.

Come follow us on instagram in the meantime!

@snowdaymagazine

Stash your phone somewhere safe and out of the way. Then, **pretend you left it at home.** You'll be amazed at how productive you can be without it! :)

>> *Andrea,*
*High School History*

One thing I do is take my laptop and work someplace where I won't be interrupted, such as a conference room. I also keep a **digital reminder list on my laptop** and my tasks appear on the day and time I have specified so I already have my priority list of what I need to accomplish that day.

>> *Virginia, Kindergarten*

I make the most of my prep or planning periods by being alert and focused. I make sure to **hydrate and eat well throughout the day so that I have the energy to get through what I need to** at school. Sometimes I get in the habit of not taking my teacher bag home to "force me" to get the work done at school. Oftentimes it is easy to believe we will prep or plan at home, only to get home and be even more unmotivated to work on school related activities.

>> *Erin,*
*Health & Phys. Ed.*

I really **don't use my planning period for planning.** Three days a week I mentor Freshmen (the other two I try to pray the rosary in the chapel).

I prefer to do my planning earlier in the morning. I get to my classroom about an hour before the students start arriving. This allows me to spend my planning period mentoring a handful of struggling students.

>> *Matthew,*
*High School History*

# PASSING

How do you make the most of your prep period?

You may delay, but time will not.
>> Benjamin Franklin

I like to turn off the lights and close the door so nobody disturbs my work time. I find it helpful to **chunk work time** as much as possible: Monday, phone calls; Tuesday, grading; Wednesday, prepping for upcoming weeks, and so on.

>> *Brittany, Middle School History*

I feel like a racehorse that is all hopped up on adrenaline by the time my conference happens. I can't focus. I know I need to grade, but I can't get in the right frame of mind. I know I need to write a test or whatever, but can't calm down enough for that either.

I usually try to xerox. Otherwise, I will tidy my room and work on my organization. Everything blows up during the day so I usually have chaos in pens, paper, and whatnot that needs to be tidied.

But, if I'm being real.... I mentally cannot handle real work on my conference. I have to **downshift, get the adrenaline out of my system** (I'm guessing it is adrenaline), and get in the right frame of mind. That can't happen until the evening. Something about my drive home allows me to transition.

>> *Laura, Secondary Science*

My desk tends to be full of post-it notes that I write on throughout the day as something comes to mind. Then during my planning period I **refer back to my notes and prioritize the things I need to accomplish.** I also have an aide, which is very helpful, and she typically makes my copies and preps the projects we have for the week while I either grade or get ready for the day's activities/lessons in the classroom.

>> *Marisa, 1st grade*

NOTES

# SPICE UP Your Coffee
## – with healthy tweaks –

*What if instead of choosing between a calorie-packed but flavorful mocha and a healthier bland coffee, you could have the best of both worlds? We've rounded up some flavorful add-ins that actually add nutrients!*

Brew your favorite blend at home, then take a large insulated carafe to school instead of your usual travel mug. You can refill a cute coffee mug right in your own classroom, without feeling rushed to drink before it gets cold. Put a small tray with your chosen coffee toppings or mix-ins on your desk, and refill your favorite homestyle mug throughout the morning.

This small shift in your daily coffee habit will make your day more relaxed and make you feel more at home.

A sprinkle of cinnamon can help lower blood glucose and triglycerides. It adds flavor and may reduce risk of cancer and heart disease, but be careful not to overdo it. Too much cinnamon can have side effecs because of the coumarin content.

A touch of cardamom can help fight off some bacterial infections, and has a healthy dose of fiber. It improves circulation and contains compounds that can fight and even prevent cancer. It's worth adding just for the added side bonus of freshening up your coffee breath!

Adding just a bit of coconut oil or coconut milk will add a nice creamy texture, and may help prevent Alzheimer's disease. It's a healthier way to add a sweet taste to your daily cup of joe and has plenty of vitamins that boost brain, bone, kidney, teeth, and heart health.

A dash of cocoa powder will help reduce your risk of heart disease, add flavor, and provide plenty of antioxidants. Dark chocolate can even protect your skin from UV rays. Either sprinkle it in as powder, or lay a small bar in the bottom of your cup and let it melt right in!

Putting a hint of cayenne into the grounds before you start brewing is not for the faint of heart, but can be worth it. Cayenne provides capsaicin, which can help manage obesity, diabetes, blood pressure, and even ulcers. Cayenne also may improve circulation and reduce headache pain.

Ginger offers digestion help, reduces inflammation, and eases symptoms of colds. It can calm a stomach and ease bloating. Add fresh ginger root by the slice right on top of your coffee beans (or grounds) before brewing, or add a hint of ginger powder instead.

Maple extract is similar to syrup, but has a lower sugar saturation, and is not as thick. Add a dash of maple extract to your coffee cup if you are on a lot of prescription medicines, because it can boost the effectiveness of your medications and will also help fight drug-resistant bacteria.

A couple of drops of hazelnut oil will add a flavor that ranks in the top few favorites among coffee lovers. Hazelnuts are packed with healthy fats, phenolic acid, fiber, and flavanols that can protect against cancer and boost overall health. They may even have anti-aging potential!

## Add a dash of flavor and a health boost at the same time!

# Coffee Add-Ins

*for pizzazz AND nutritional value*

## best of both worlds

Vanilla has many benefits, and can be added in pure extract form, or by adding vanilla beans right into the coffee grounds. Here's what vanilla can do for your mind and body:

- boost mental performance
- improve metabolism
- calm stomach aches
- eliminate free radicals
- reduce joint pain
- regulate heart rate
- improve brain health
- lower cholesterol
- relieve stress
- regulate blood pressure
- cure male impotency
- alleviate arthritis and gout
- aid the immune system with antioxidants
- boost mood

Use real cream instead of processed creamer. Ideally, look for full-fat cream from grass fed cows. If you like the type with added flavors, try using real organic extracts for taste. You'll get calcium and vitamin K instead of the suspicious ingredients in an artificial creamer.

Grow a stevia plant in your home. It's a calorie-free alternative to sugar. You can drop a leaf or two right in your cup of hot tea or coffee, or you can easily create a dry powder, just like you buy in a packet. Just harvest and wash the leaves of your stevia plant and leave them to dry for a day or so. They will become crunchy and easy to crush into a sweetener that you can sprinkle in foods or drinks!

*loving snowday? snap a pic and share on social*

You may already be aware that coffee drinkers have an increased lifespan, but now we know even more promising health facts.

# Water and Coffee by the Numbers

Each daily cup of coffee has been linked to a 7% reduced risk of type 2 diabetes. For example, three cups per day lowers risk by 21%!

Drinking coffee helps lower risk of heart disease and stroke.

Drinking coffee regularly decreases risk for liver cirrhosis and liver cancer.

Regular coffee drinkers have as much as a 65% decreased risk of Alzheimer's and Parkinson's disease.

Women who drink coffee are less likely to suffer from depression.

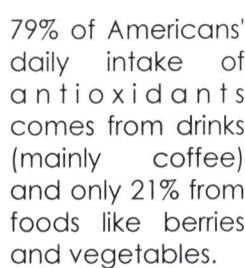

**TOTAL DAILY ANTIOXIDANT INTAKE**

79% of Americans' daily intake of antioxidants comes from drinks (mainly coffee) and only 21% from foods like berries and vegetables.

**RECOMMENDED**

**ACTUAL**

On average, American adults drink 39 ounces of water each day.

The recommended minimum is 64 ounces of water per day, but more hydration is required if you are exercising, breastfeeding, or pregnant, and needs vary by sex, age, and environment.

Sources: Healthline, CDC

Only 22% of adults drink the recommended 8 glasses of water each day. 7% reported no water intake at all on an average day!

About half the adults in the U.S. drink coffee every day. Of those coffee drinkers, the average intake is 3.5 cups.

4-6 cups of coffee a day can be safe, but be careful- That advice is based on an 8 ounce cup. Many of our mugs are larger than that.

**QUIT COFFEE INTAKE AT 3PM TO AVOID IMPACTING YOUR SLEEP.**

It's hard to stay hydrated and energized all day. You may be used to sneaking sips of cold black coffee from your travel mug after forgetting to take attendance. And you know that the occasional dash to refill your water bottle never feels appealing. Ditch the same old boring drinks, and add some spice to your daily life! Most of us go between water and coffee throughout the day, without straying from our go-to flavorings.

These twists on your daily drink staples will help you get the flavor you crave while keeping your nutritional needs in mind! Certain spices, oils, and plants are delicious when added to coffee and also add health benefits. And infused water is a great way to sneak in a few extra nutrients while staying hydrated. Choose your favorite recipes, or mix and match to blend your own new brands of daily drinks! Having a fun new taste to reach for will make you more likely to keep up with your mug or bottle all day long. Just be warned - your friends will be begging you to make a larger batch for the teachers' lounge before long.

YOUR ALL-DAY DRINKING

# WATER & COFFEE

## Having trouble sneaking in your 8 glasses a day?

Increase your hydration, and soak up a few extra nutrients with infused water. Switching up the flavors will keep you coming back for more, and you'll avoid the sugars and the artificial ingredients hiding in the flavored drinks available at the store.

*Water is life's matter and matrix, mother and medium. There is no life without water. >> Albert Szent-Gyorgyi, M.D.*

# INFUSE
*your water with tasty nutrients*

## How much water do you actually drink each day?

Here are the stats.

> People are finally starting to eliminate soda and drink more water. In 1998, Americans drank an average of 54 gallons of soda and 42 gallons of water (per person, each year). In 2013 the numbers had shifted to 44 gallons of soda and 58 gallons of water.

> However, that is still only about 2.5 glasses per day on average! We need to continue increasing our daily water intake goals.

> Now, the general recommendation is to try to drink 2-3 cups of water per hour, and more if you are sweating.

## Is there such a thing as OVER-hydrating?

Actually, yes! But it takes a lot. Your kidneys can process around 6 gallons per day. The key, though, is to spread out your drinking. The body can generally handle quite a bit of water as long as you don't surpass a liter in an hour. You'd have to be drinking at a fast rate over a short period of time to actually suffer from water intoxication.

orange

rosemary
>>> tart
>>> bitter
>>> sour

grapefruit

Use cold or room temperature water, and then refrigerate for an hour or two, or add ice.

## chopping guide

When working with hard fruits that are less juicy, cut them into very thin slices. This applies to apples, pears, peaches, and even ginger. Ginger should be peeled first.

Citrus fruits can be cut into slices or into wedges. Even quarters are sometimes enough. If you will be drinking the infused water fairly quickly, keep the peel on. If you'll be waiting more than 6 hours, you may want to peel your citrus first. The zestier outside may cause your water to become bitter over time. This applies to lemon, lime, orange, and grapefruit.

For herbs, crush with a spoon, muddler, mortar and pestle, or even with your knife instead of cutting.

If you include smaller pieces, like spices, edible flower petals, or loose herbs, you may want to gather them into a tea ball or infuser to get flavor without dregs.

After 24 hours, strain out any solid material. Keep refrigerated and use the water within a few days for safety.

Select organic ingredients when you can. Wash all your produce before cutting.

Avoid using hot water, since it may cause some of the ingredients to melt a bit or fall apart.

Hot water also can decrease the effect of the nutrients.

Once you have everything ready, use the chopping guide and the soaking guide for your chosen ingredients.

## soaking guide

If you want to drink your infused water immediately, try using ingredients that do not require a lot of soak time. These include:
>>> watermelon
>>> mint
>>> crushed berries
>>> sliced cucumber
>>> unpeeled lime
>>> oranges
>>> cantaloupe
>>> grapefruit

When you plan to drink your water within the first few hours after preparing it, you can also infuse with:
>>> strawberries
>>> kiwi
>>> halved blueberries

For water you will infuse today, but drink tomorrow, use these foods that taste best after an overnight soak:
>>> apples
>>> pears
>>> cinnamon
>>> thyme
>>> rosemary
>>> ginger

If you are aiming for long-term good looks for an infused drink to serve at tomorrow's party, stick with long soakers, like the following:
>>> whole berries
>>> peeled lemons
>>> oranges
>>> herbs that are not crushed

exploring the endless potential of paper crafting

# Paper's Possibilities

1 >> There are many uses for low-tech pop-ups. Try tinkerlab.com or personalcreations.com for guidance.

2 >> Tutorials on YouTube show how to fold origami paper heart boxes.

3 >> Next time you study an animal, or life cycle, have students create a 3d model for labeling instead of just a flat page. Some incredible interactive paper dissection models are available online as well.

4 >> Print templates that combine art and math. Create decorations, tabletop sports, and more using free printable nets from polyhedra.net

5 >> Create a mood book that represents your goals, memories, and dreams for the year.

6 >> Hide feedback for students or clues for a scavenger hunt inside themed paper containers.

7 >> Create a classroom tree with paper ornaments that represent the variety of topics you've covered this year.

8 >> If students plot everything correctly, these graphs transform into paper airplanes when they fold on the lines. (available from Math Giraffe)

9 >> Recycle magazine pages into beautiful creations.

10 >> Save odds and ends of pretty packaging from deliveries to make a craft station.

11 >> Learn the art of paper quilling as your next hobby. Get inspired with patterns for beginners at thesprucecrafts.com

12 >> Fold cardstock into "pockets" for interactive notebook pieces.

13 >> Patterned scrapbook paper makes it easy for kids' creations to look pro-level with just a tracing template and scissors.

14 >> Find a local origami group or take a class with origamiusa.org

15 >> Kids love all things huge and all things tiny. Help them make and customize teeny little notebooks for a special unit of study coming up.

*You can't use up creativity. The more you use, the more you have.* >> Maya Angelou

# A Creative Teacher Masters the Art of Papercrafting

text and photos by Hanna of "hanakrafts"
Find hanakrafts on instagram and at hanakrafts.com

High School English & Lit Teacher  
Papercrafter  
Bookbinder

# HANNA MARYAM
@hanakrafts

**I want to show the beauty of Asian designs to the world, through the medium of paper.**

I'm Hanna and I'm the owner and solo maker behind hanakrafts. I sell handmade paper products that feature traditional Asian designs, and some of the goods that I make are gift envelopes, greeting cards and notecard sets. I also do bookbinding and enjoy making notebooks and journals. In my other life, I'm a full-time English and Literature teacher at a high school in Singapore. This is my tenth year in teaching and my fourth year doing hanakrafts!

I started hanakrafts in 2015, when my husband and I were making a big move to New Zealand. He had found a job there, but I knew it would be pretty hard for me to find a teaching job, because you need a local qualification to teach in NZ. So that's when I was inspired to do something completely different and decided to start up my own handmade business that would allow me to sell online! Because I wasn't working, I could really devote all of my time to developing the business—coming up with new product ideas, working on my website and Etsy shop, improving my product photography, and diversifying my business by doing markets and conducting workshops. In 2017, we moved back to Singapore, and I was in two minds about continuing with hanakrafts, but my husband convinced me to carry on with it. Two years on I must say that was a good decision because I've really seen the business grow!

When I was 11, I was selected for a school exchange programme to Japan, and that was where my host family first introduced me to origami paper. I loved how beautiful and delicate these papers were, and I especially loved the texture of washi paper and yuzen chiyogami paper. Since then, I've always loved all things Japanese, and when I was thinking of starting my handmade business, I went right back to that memory of discovering the beautiful origami paper all those years ago. It inspired me to focus on incorporating traditional Asian designs into my craft.

# Ideas & Inspiration from Hanna

I read magazines like Real Simple and Flow to look for inspiration, and I also love finding new prints and patterns to work with at hole-in-the-wall shops.

I can never find the time to read, so now what I do every Saturday morning is to reach for a book on my bedside table the minute I wake up. It's worked pretty well for me so far!

Balancing work, teaching, and life:

It's tough, honestly! Teaching is a truly fulfilling job, but it takes up so much of you emotionally, mentally and physically every day, that by the time I get home, I'm just exhausted. I try to give myself a little break every weekend doing something entirely unrelated to work or my business - going out for a movie or shopping at a local market with my husband are my favourite activities to do!

Favorite Book:

The Buried Giant by Kazuo Ishiguro

## Finding Time and Space to Create

Because school ends early on Fridays, I usually spend a few hours in the afternoon in my home studio making and designing future collections. I also ensure that I plan my time out for those precious hours so that I don't get carried away and end up doing nothing!

I have a spare room that I use as a home studio, and that's where I've got my work desk, my printer, my packaging area, and all of my beautiful paper materials. It has a view of a small hill at the back of my high-rise flat, but most of the time I keep my windows shut because the air-conditioning is on when I'm working! Singapore is really hot and humid and I need to keep the room cool to preserve my paper.

You can be inspired anywhere and anytime, so be ready when it strikes! I've found that it helps to keep a little notebook handy just to jot down your ideas. Also, it doesn't matter if you have a whole day, or a few hours, or just 30 minutes to spare for creative work -- do a little bit consistently and it will all add up.

## Try Bookbinding in Your Classroom

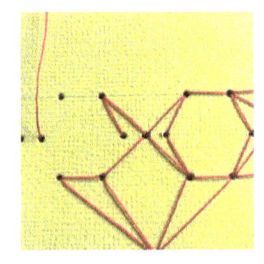

Ditch the plastic binding when compiling students' work. Try a design using an awl, needle, and thread!

# 5 TIPS

## for starting a crafty side gig

1 >> Be clear about what product/service you want to offer and how you stand out from the rest.

2 >> Tell your family and friends so that they can support you and spread the word.

3 >> At the start, always have something new to launch or to introduce to your audience. For me, I launched a new gift envelope design every week in the first few months of my business, and this helped to attract attention to what I was doing.

4 >> Focus on one sales channel and one social media platform first—you can always have more later.

5 >> Make sure you can devote at least a few hours every week to working on the side hustle, and good luck!

## While You Work...

Podcasts to Inspire Creative Endeavors
>> The Business of Making
>> Create and Thrive
>> The Product Boss

## Teachers,

When the going gets tough (and it always will!), just remember that one kid who told you how you made a difference in his life, or how you made him believe in himself again, or simply how you helped him to understand something in class more clearly. That one kid will teach you more about yourself than you know.
Also: done is better than perfect!

Find Hanna's handmade journals, cards, and envelopes at hanakrafts.com

# WORDS
## with beauty

THESE LOVELY TERMS FROM DIFFERENT CULTURES DESCRIBE WHAT WE HAVE NEVER QUITE FOUND THE WORDS TO SAY.

### MERAKI
#### Greek
(verb): leaving a piece of your creative soul behind in your work, thereby passing on the love you poured into it

### KAUKOKAIPUU
#### Finnish
(noun): a deep desire to travel to far-off places, a craving, or even homesick feeling for a land you've never even seen

# LIVSNJUTARE

Swedish

(noun): someone who loves life deeply
and lives it to the extreme

CHERISH YOUR VISIONS AND YOUR DREAMS AS THEY ARE THE CHILDREN OF YOUR SOUL, THE BLUEPRINTS OF YOUR ULTIMATE ACHIEVEMENTS.
>> NAPOLEON HILL

# UBUNTU

### Zulu

(noun): the belief that the universal bond of humanity is rooted in compassion and kindness

## BOKETTO

**Japanese**

(noun): the act of gazing absentmindedly into the distance

## DADIRRI

**Aboriginal**

(noun): the practice of deep listening in the beauty and stillness of nature, reflecting on nature, inner spirit, and God's creation

## HULYA

**Turkish**

(noun): a daydream that brings happiness

## YUGEN

**Japanese**

(noun): a profound emotional response upon realizing the level of depth, mystery, and beauty of the universe

## POCHEMUCHKA

Russian

(noun): a child who asks a lot of questions

## JAYUS

Indonesian

(noun): a joke so unfunny and poorly told that you cannot help but laugh

## RASTROPHILIOPUSTROCITY

English

(noun): an ignition of a creative spark, immediately followed by inspired action to bring the idea forth into existence

## CHINGHOTIYAAN

Urdu

(noun): the messy, but careful handwriting of small children still learning to write

ARE YOU THE KIND OF TEACHER WHO LOVES WORDS LIKE "SHENANIGANS" AND "LOLLYGAGGING?" THEN YOU'LL WANT TO SAVE THESE NEW WORDS TO USE AT SCHOOL!

## LUFTMENSCH

### Yiddish

(noun): someone who is impractical, or a bit of a dreamer (head in the clouds), literally, "air person"

## HABSELIGKEITEN

### German

(noun): a collection of items that looks like worthless junk to an adult, but is precious treasure to children

## LAGOM

### Swedish

(noun): just the right amount for moderation, a sufficient and suitable balance without overdoing it

# Getting Started with dry brushing

## body brushing for skin health

Dry skin brushing has been practiced for centuries as a way to remove dead skin and improve circulation. Many cultures, including the ancient Greeks and Egyptians discovered its benefits.

Exfoliating skin, the largest organ in the body, with the stiff bristles of a body brush can offer some appealing results:

>> **reduce the appearance of cellulite**
>> **give skin a healthy glow**
>> **stimulate nerves, leading to alertness and energy**
>> **smooth rough skin**
>> **aid in relaxation**
>> **potentially stimulate lymphatic flow**

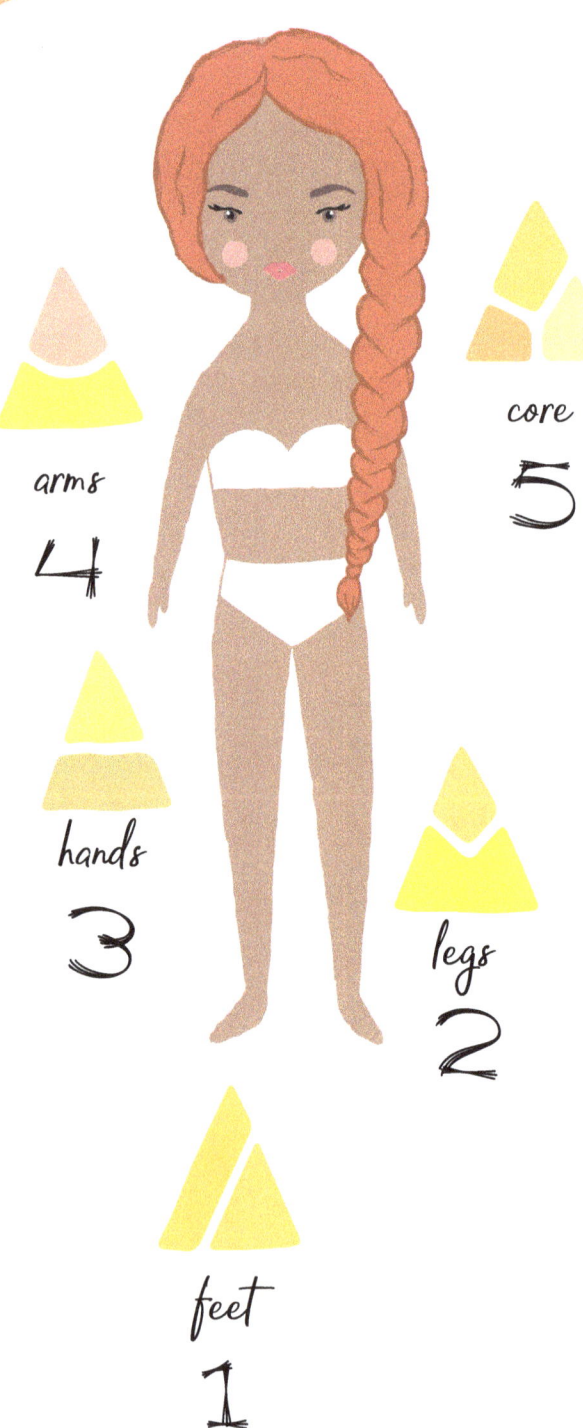

arms 4
core 5
hands 3
legs 2
feet 1

*Try adding a bit of cypress essential oil for a pleasant scent and improved circulation. Put a few drops in the palm of your hand, and brush across the oil to apply it to your dry brush before starting.*

Use a brush designed specifically for skin, and only brush when your body is dry. Morning is the best time for your dry brush routine. Find a comfortable, quiet space to enjoy and relax, as you would for a foot massage.

Use light pressure in areas with thin skin. On elbows, knees, and the bottoms of your feet, you can apply a bit more pressure, but keep the brushing gentle. It should cause a bit of friction, but not hurt.

1. Begin with the soles of the feet. Brush in circles, 10-15 times around per foot. Move on to the tops of the feet. Continue in wide, circular motions.

2. Brush upwards from the ankles, slowly moving up the legs. Always keep motions directed toward the heart. Rough dry skin on knees and elbows may need extra attention with the brush.

3. Once you finish lower extremities, move to the hands. Brush palms 10-15 times in a circular motion.

4. Next, raise one arm at a time. Brush down toward the heart, moving gradually from the wrists to the armpits, and finishing with the shoulders.

5. Brush the neck, abdomen, back, and shoulders. Avoid the more sensitive areas of the body.

Shower afterward. The exfoliating effect requires that you rinse off dead skin cells gently with warm water. Skin can become more sensitive after brushing. Use moisturizer with natural oils to re-moisturize your skin.

*invigorate    exfoliate    refresh*

## how to get the brushed - skin glow safely

Brush gently. The process should never be painful.

Avoid broken or bruised skin, nipples, and any sensitive areas.

Always brush from the extremities toward the heart for circulation.

Use a natural fiber brush designed specifically for dry skin brushing.

If you plan to brush your face, you'll need a second, softer brush, since facial skin is more tender.

To avoid irritation, do not practice dry brushing more than once a week.

Consult a doctor before attempting if you have any conditions, and do not brush your skin if you suffer from eczema or psoriasis.

To avoid infection, do not share your brush.

Clean your brush periodically, but be sure it dries out completely before its next use.

# 5 Ways to Style a
# MAXI DRESS

Carmen Myer
@thelylasblog

Spring is here! While dressing for Fall is collectively everyone's favorite, and there's a special glamour added to Winter due to the endless holiday parties, it's a relief when the warmer weather of Spring rolls around. This means bright patterns and colors, an array of florals, warm-toned manicures and if you're like me, the return of the maxi dress. As a teacher, the maxi dress is one of my wardrobe staples. It checks all the boxes: work appropriate, comfortable and stylish. Check, check, check. While they are a lifesaver when we feel like we have nothing else to wear, these dresses can also feel a bit monotonous. That's where I want to help you. There's no reason to feel like you are becoming bored with your wardrobe. It's time to think outside of those boxes and utilize the different pieces we have in our closets. This saves money and gets our creativity flowing outside of those classroom walls. Here are five different ways anyone can elevate a simple maxi dress with items you currently own!

*Rock a jean jacket*

Simple and easy. A jean jacket, some sunnies, and a simple necklace go a long way. I feel like this gives off such a cool, modern vibe while making your maxi dress feel less like a homeschooler from the 90's.

*Throw on a scarf*

What's better than color?... more color! Don't shy away from adding a fun scarf to a solid colored dress. Bonus points if you belt it, adding more dimension to your outfit, and your scarf won't be in your way!

*Never say no to a kimono*

How do you get California style while living in Louisiana? Just add a lightweight kimono-esque top! I love this outfit so much I wore it after school to a party, and will probably wear it many more times this summer. Mine was from Target last year, but hopefully this is the type of item you already have in your closet as well!

**4** It's 2020 and vests are here to stay. Whether it be a waterfall vest from 2015 like mine, or a jean vest you have from H&M, either will look great layered with a maxi dress.

Try a simple vest

5 — Chambray shirts are basic, but in the most glorious way possible. They literally go well with anything, and they are teacher, mom, and women everywhere approved. You could leave this unknotted and unbuttoned, but I like giving my waist a little bit more definition by buttoning the shirt halfway and then tying it.

# teacher BAKER CREATOR

Weekdays are for school.

Saturdays are for sugared delights.

Sundays are for me.

photos and text by Shannon O'Connor
@teacherbakercreator

Hello there! I am Shannon, a 3rd year teacher lucky enough to be living and teaching up in sunny, beautiful Broome. I was born in Darwin and have lived in 4 different states/territories as I grew up. Not just a one trick pony over here- I also bake! On the side, you'll catch me on the weekend in the kitchen whipping up and taste testing all of the sweet treats or down at the beach with friends. Cakes, donuts and slices are my specialty.

Always carry a set of cutlery. You never know when the opportunity to snack may arise.

### Self Care Strategy:

Well it helps when you live 300m from one the best beaches in the world! Is it too corny to say long sunset walks on the beach?!

Broome is such a diverse and welcoming little town to teach in. Trans-generational trauma is a huge factor for a lot of our kids and all the schools in the area (and surrounds) are working so hard with families and community groups/agencies to help support our kids in the best possible ways.

### Favorite Lunch to Pack for School:

Definitely left overs from dinner the night before- there is no time to be messing around with anything too gourmet for me. I am a bit of a self-professed snack queen, so baked treats, fruit and lots of dip are my go-to. I love a good dip, vegetable and cheese for recess.

### Mental Health Checks

My kiddies complete a mental health check in every morning and after breaks which we adore and have come to learn lots about this year in Year 5.

I am so lucky to work in possibly the greatest school ever in terms of support. We are a trauma informed and PBS (Positive Behaviour Support) school so nearly everything we do at my school is focussed on student centred learning.

We work to teach positive behaviours, including learning to self regulate and self care. My aim is to create a nurturing and safe space the kids love and feel a part of. Try the playlist "Hey Kids, calm Down" by Zoe Foster Blake on Spotify. This playlist brings so much joy into my classroom.

### Morning Routine:

**4.45am**
Struggle to wake up

**4.55am**
Actually get out of bed and get ready for the gym

**5.30am**
Gym

**6.20am**
Get home, quickly shower, get changed and make a smoothie

**6.40am**
Grab the food scraps for the chickens at school and head to school

**6.45am**
Arrive at school and sort myself for the day/week

**7.30am**
School starts... bring on the madness!

### Teacher Clothes:

I'm all about the bright patterns and anything light and flowy for sweaty Broome. Too much money is spent on online shopping in my house (SELF CARE, right?!)

### Favorite Corner of the Classroom:

So many comfy learning spaces to choose from! I am all about flexible learning spaces and the kids making great learning decisions when choosing spots to work and who to work with. The kids and I both do love my 'LOOK WHAT I'VE LEARNT' wall at the back of our classroom. The kids are so proud of displaying work on the wall and explaining all the wonderful learning they did to produce that piece of work. What superstars!

Follow Shannon
@teacherbakercreator

### Teacher Tip:

Always have a stash of lollies/chocolates readily available in the cupboard in case of emergency- for the kids, support staff or yourself!

### What fills your soul?

dad jokes and hot chips

### Wellness:

Although I hate getting out of bed for it, going to the gym in the morning does set me up for a great day!

**Favorite Instagram Accounts to Follow:**

@cgsteachinginsta

This lady knows how to rock a colourful classroom with all the fun and engaging activities! So many fab and innovative classroom ideas. This instagram gives me all the inspiration!

@missjorjesclassroom

Graduate teacher also up in Broome, and best girl ever! Love her fantastic honest insights. All around great gal to get on board with.

I am all about working hard on the weekdays to make the most of my weekends. And by that I mean baking cakes. It's all about balance. Summer holidays, my priorities are travelling and going to the nearest Kmart to stock up on goodies.

*You might be the only positive thing in a child's day, so make every second count.*

**5 tips for a a great Swiss Meringue:**

1. Get yourself down to Bunnings and get a plasterer's scraper (taping knife). It will make your meringue so much smoother on the cake then any cake tool will give you! Honestly, life changing.

2. Lurpak butter is my go-to brand, for light coloured and fluffy icing. Does not get any better.

3. Refrigerate your cakes before icing. It will make the world of difference and stop those pesky crumbs making their way into the icing.

4. Rub the meringue mix in between two fingers to make sure it is a smooth consistency and all the sugar is dissolved correctly before beating

5. Taste test of course!

Make your classroom work for you and your kids. Trial and test new things out. Use the environment that you are in as a third teacher, make it work for you and your kiddies and if in doubt, print on coloured paper.

*Making cakes is such a great creative hobby. It doesn't matter if it looks great or not; everyone loves cake.*

**How do you manage slow living, and taking breaks from your phone when you need to?**

Term time is my own time. I work pretty hard during the term doing all sorts of things at school and for school as well as baking on the weekends. My school holidays are my down time. Thanks to all the tech overlords at Apple for introducing Screen Time. Life and time saver for me!

**What are you most grateful for?**
Fab friends and my Kitchenaid.

**What are you most passionate about?**
Quality education and great tasting food...can you tell?

**Book Recommendation:**

The Prettiest Horse in the Glue Factory by Corey White. Such a moving memoir of trauma, survival and the importance of education.

# THE *hands* OF A TEACHER

Brigid Danziger

>>>>>>>>>>>>>

Take a moment to reflect on the many things your hands do all day. Just look down and appreciate them. Admire the way that your hands were created to move in so many ways to do everything that is vital to your daily activities.

You know the backs of your own hands, but do you ever think about how often your students look at your hands? They watch them all day, and get up-close looks when you help them one on one.

If I stop to reflect on the hands of the people I love most, I realize how well I know those hands. My mom's hands have always looked like the embodiment of love to me. I can visualize the strong veins in her hands, and the way her ring spins and slides around because her fingers are so thin, but her knuckles are so big.

I smile when I picture my husband's strong hands. I think of the way they massage my shoulders after a long day, and the way they are all nicked up and often bloody from woodworking. Those hands have brought such beauty and happiness to our home, by building furniture, giving baby baths, chopping herbs, and holding my own hand.

You can probably stop and imagine your favorite teacher, and still picture her hands. You may remember them resting gently on your arm as a reminder or you may remember them holding your own hand around your pencil to show you exactly how to do something. Can you remember the way the skin on those hands looked, or what rings she wore?

Our hands bring such joy to the world by small, continued actions. Consider everything your hands did just during the last school day alone. Those actions build up to shape a year's worth of teaching, over and over again.

Our hands are critical to our work. Each pair of teacher hands has its own story and has contributed to a great journey. Appreciate the potential of your own hands! What will they do next?

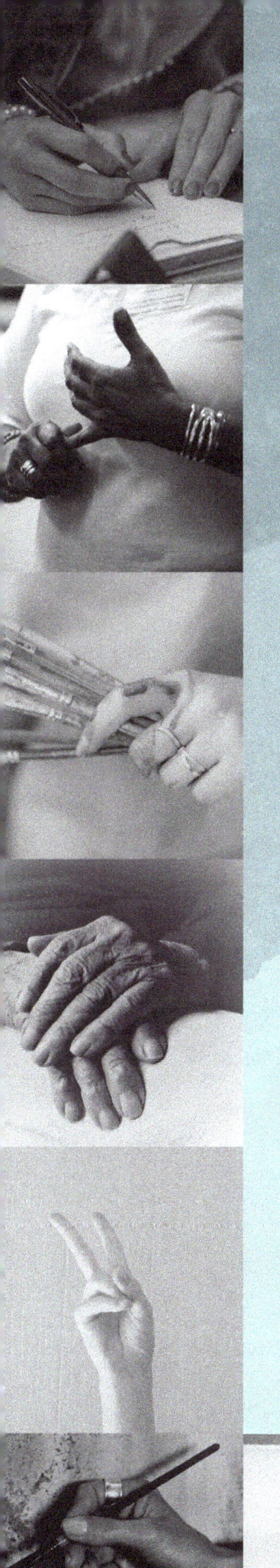

The hands of a teacher wipe.
Wiping whiteboards clean,
wiping noses dry,
and wiping tears away.

The hands of a teacher build.
Building bridges, robots, and towers for STEM challenges,
building relationships with parents,
and building futures.

The hands of a teacher collect.
Collecting more papers to grade,
collecting stains and paint spatters on the skin,
collecting glitter that will never come off,
and collecting germs.

The hands of a teacher wiggle.
Wiggling loose a stubborn locker latch that just won't budge,
wiggling in the air to emphatically demonstrate a new science concept,
and wiggling toward each bus window to wave goodbye on dismissal duty.

The hands of a teacher hold.
Holding little hands on a field trip, holding twelve jackets and four pairs of
mittens cast aside excitedly at recess on the first warm day of spring, and
eventually holding the door for a long, proud line of graduates.

The hands of a teacher turn.
Turning to crank the pencil sharpener until they blister,
turning to flip each chair up onto the desk after a rushed dismissal,
and even turning the door knob to lock down the classroom, securing the
room in preparation for the worst.

The hands of a teacher cup the face of a hanging head that droops to fall
asleep on the stack of papers yet to be graded.
The hands of a teacher fold together to pray for each child that needs
guidance or has an unhappy home.
The hands of a teacher wring together, worn out with worry.

But the next morning...
The hands of a teacher warm themselves around a cup of coffee, hoist up a
heavy teacher bag, and move quickly to gather up materials.

Filled with hope again, and ready to offer themselves for another beautiful
day of guiding, loving, and teaching.

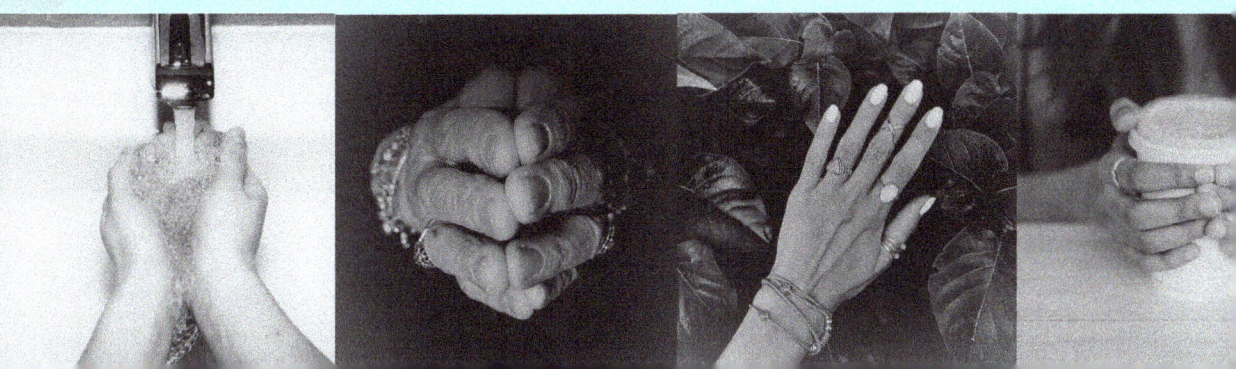

# WHAT WILL FUEL YOUR SOUL NEXT?

## A "HOBBY HEALTH" EXERCISE

### Time for a checkup!

Assess your self-interests using this exercise. First, reflect on your seasons of life, represented in your activities throughout your journey so far. Color what you have dabbled in (tried even just once) with one color, what you used to do regularly in another, and what you currently do in a third color. Often we lose a passion or set aside a hobby, sometimes without even realizing it has drifted away. In each fresh season of life, new adventures await us. Old activities that used to be out of reach, due to finance, ages of children, or other limitations, may now become possible. Others no longer feel rewarding, or become less accessible with age or scheduling challenges. Take time to re-evaluate what activities are no longer working for you, and which are your strongest passions.

*color is the keyboard, the eyes are the harmonies, the soul is the piano with many strings. the artist is the hand that plays, touching one key or another, to cause vibrations in the soul*
>> *wassily kandinsky*

### What will you do next?

Now, look at the icons that are not colored, one at a time. Go very slowly, and actually visualize yourself doing each one. What feeling does it bring to mind? Do you imagine yourself being fulfilled by it? Excited? Peaceful? Intrigued? Proud? Soothed? Is that what you need in this season of life? You might surprise yourself as you highlight with one last color what you may consider trying next!

YES, YOU DO HAVE TIME TO PRIORITIZE YOUR INTERESTS! DO NOT RUSH, OR PASS OVER ICONS THAT YOU HAVE NOT CONSIDERED BEFORE. TAKE A MOMENT TO IMAGINE HOW EACH SQUARE WOULD IMPACT YOU. LET YOUR MIND "TRY ON" EACH ONE!

### Reflect on what you want to focus on.

How will your prioritize it? Journal about this exercise and what strategies you will put in place to ensure that this new hobby or interest happens for you.

DURING THIS EXERCISE, YOU ARE LIKELY TO HAVE OLD MEMORIES ARISE FOR CERTAIN ACTIVITIES. IF YOU HAVE A "OH WOW, HOW I USED TO LOVE THAT" MOMENT, CALL A FRIEND WHO ENJOYED IT WITH YOU TO RECONNECT AND REMINISCE ABOUT IT.

# Productivity Chart
*strategically coordinate your tasks with your cycle*

Re-organize your to-do list into this calendar. Consider where each task belongs, and your productivity levels will start to soar!

| cycle day 1 | cycle day 2 | cycle day 3 | cycle day 4 | cycle day 5 | cycle day 6 | cycle day 7 | *creativity* |
|---|---|---|---|---|---|---|---|
| cycle day 8 | cycle day 9 | cycle day 10 | cycle day 11 | cycle day 12 | cycle day 13 | cycle day 14 | *communication* |
| cycle day 15 | cycle day 16 | cycle day 17 | cycle day 18 | cycle day 19 | cycle day 20 | cycle day 21 | *focus* |
| cycle day 22 | cycle day 23 | cycle day 24 | cycle day 25 | cycle day 26 | cycle day 27 | cycle day 28 | *reflection* |

**copy me!**

Use p. 56-59 for reference.
Enter normal calendar dates in the circles.

# Inspiration from..

## Mother Teresa

"Do not allow yourselves to be disheartened by any failure as long as you have done your best."

### the people closest to us

"It is easy to love the people far away. It is not always easy to love those close to us. It is easier to give a cup of rice to relieve hunger than to relieve the loneliness and pain of someone unloved in our own home. Bring love into your home for this is where our love for each other must start."

### do it with great love

"It is not the magnitude of our actions but the amount of love that is put into them that matters."

"There is more hunger for love and appreciation in this world than for bread."

*Let us always meet each other with a smile for the smile is the beginning of love.*

### we belong to each other

"If we have no peace, it is because we have forgotten that we belong to each other."

"The success of love is in the loving – it is not in the result of loving. Of course it is natural in love to want the best for the other person, but whether it turns out that way or not does NOT determine the value of what we have done."

Quotes from Mother Teresa

www.ingramcontent.com/pod-product-compliance
Lightning Source LLC
Chambersburg PA
CBHW061153070526
44584CB00034B/4500